THE PARENT TRACK

Christine Sandman Stone

The Parent Track

Work-Life Balance Hacks to Elevate Your Career and Raise Good Humans

ISBN 13: 978-1-63489-293-3
Library of Congress Catalog Number: 2019919139
Printed in the United States of America
First Printing: 2020

24   23 22 21   20   5   4   3   2   1

Cover design by Steve Leard
Interior design by Jack Walgamuth

Wise Ink Creative Publishing
807 Broadway St NE
Suite 46
Minneapolis, MN, 55413

To order, visit www.itascabooks.com or call 1-800-901-3480.
Reseller discounts available.

To change, growth, love, and progress.

Dear Doloni & Marina

I hope you find
some great ideas to
help with Zoe!
with so much love!
Mom

CONTENTS

ACKNOWLEDGMENTS

Each week, I reflect on what I am grateful for. These folks have made the list many times:

For my mom, Judy, who is the queen of hacks and laughter. For my dad, Jack, who is my first mentor and will still talk for hours about challenges and possibilities.

For the circle of mentees and mentors in my life: I learn so much from you, and I am elevated by being part of our communities. I am especially grateful for Megan, Leslie, Jane, and John, who champion women in technology in Chicago. Your organizations have made such an impact for me and for others.

For my teams that have made work fun and remarkable. For my wise bosses. From my exceptional bosses who were strong teachers, I learned that the gift of a well-taught skill lasts and amplifies.

I am particularly grateful to Tom and Andrew who taught me how to assess technology projects and predict their impact and costs, Gary who gave great counsel on how to adapt when leading people, Ed who shared how to build high-performing teams, and Deb who shared how to approach, lead, and measure innovation and build a cohort of women leaders around you.

For my friends, siblings, neighbors, book clubs, euchre group, women I exercise with, and our support network who have helped me navigate through busy times.

There is a saying that you can't be what you can't see. To women leaders I have worked with: people see you, I see you, and it changes the game.

For my female peers: the power of your smarts and your encouragement puts fuel in my proverbial tank—in particular: Kristy, Kim, Julie, Sara, MaryKay, Lisa, and Gretchen.

For everyone who has been honest in a tough situation: your insight has been a huge help. For everyone who has helped me brainstorm: I am smarter with your challenging questions. For everyone who smiled at me or said something kind about how my work helped you: I have saved your smile and words, and they have energized me.

For Jim: may I laugh with you for another thirty years. You have helped me reset and refocus in my work more times than we can count. You are my top adviser.

For my children: thank you for proofreading, talking about theory, and being quiet when I was on conference calls. I love to watch you thrive as grown-ups; it's pretty nifty.

You are all a gift to me.

INTRODUCTION

Our women's network was excited. We had gotten the most senior woman in our organization—let's call her Susan—to come speak at our first networking event over Women's Day. Unlike many of my colleagues, I had already met her.

Not long before our event, I traveled to our company's headquarters for an unrelated meeting, where our paths crossed for the first time. I made a point to introduce myself in the reception area, and Susan invited me into her office.

She was the first woman to become part of the executive group, and I was excited to meet her. I hoped that her hiring would mean more opportunities for me and the women in my division. I had been doing top-notch work, and my projects were fairly well known even at the corporate office. I wanted to make a good impression and have her agree to come and speak to our newly formed women's network.

Susan made an amazing first impression on me. She was polished and professional; her suit was perfect, and her tone was welcoming. We found a quick rapport, talking about our backgrounds and, in time, turning to more personal details. I knew she had relocated from a different state, and I asked where she was living. She told me about her new home and how her husband had relocated to a local branch of his law firm. I casually asked, "Do you have any children?"

1

She crossed her legs, paused, and said, "Oh no." She leaned in as if sharing a deeply valuable insight and declared, "I have never met a successful woman in business who has children."

At the time, I had four children under ten and, throughout our conversation, had been hoping like hell that I didn't have Cheerios stuck to the back of my skirt.

After Susan's declaration, I took a deep breath, turned the conversation to the upcoming Women's Day celebration, and asked her if she would come speak. I never offered any details about my personal life, and she didn't ask.

Flash forward a month, and I was supposed to go to the airport to pick up Susan. That morning, I discovered that my youngest—Will, who had never had a sick visit with the doctor—suddenly had a solid fever. Not one of those "I can ignore it and send him to preschool" fevers, but an "any parent can recognize this kid is a germ factory from fifty feet away" fever. My husband Jim was on the road, so I was on my own. My friend Janet had two daughters my kids' ages, and I called her in tears. Her youngest was also sick, and since we had the same pediatrician, she volunteered to pick up Will and his insurance card and to do a twofer at the doctor.

I drove to O'Hare airport, picked up Susan, drove her to our office, and introduced her to the crowd of four hundred women who had come to hear her speak. She then went off to a dinner engagement. While I was with Susan, Janet took Will to the doctor, stopped at the pharmacy, and had him started on antibiotics before I even got home.

I drove home in tears, and that night I fell asleep holding Will. I felt like a failure. How could I choose Susan—a woman who had a clear and publicly shared bias against working parents—instead of spending time with my sick three-year-old? I was torn. I knew the career cost to me would be high if I missed picking her up and introducing her because I had a sick child. But still I wondered what kind of parent I was to not be with my child.

The truth is that rarely, but sometimes, there are battles we can't win. In my dreams, I hoped Susan would get to know me and realize that working parents could be impactful and essential to their teams, but I was certain I was never going to help her shift her entire perspective about working parents in the small window of time she knew me.

Failing would have perhaps hurt my career and others who worked for her later. I chose my battle. I chose to show up at work and give it my all. My choice wasn't ideal—I thought about my child the entire day—but in the end, we all survived.

To this day, Janet and her family are still dear to us. They live in a rural area, so I have repaid her friendship with years of hosting trick-or-treating and bike-riding adventures on our sidewalks, two things her girls couldn't do on their ranch.

Today, Will is a lanky, healthy young man who has no memory of that eventful day in our lives. For me, though, the impact was significant. I became more guarded about talking about family, but I also became even more certain that I didn't want to slide into a life where I took better care of the Susans in my career than my own family.

Finding a way to make things work isn't always elegant. My husband Jim and I don't have Ivy League degrees, a lot of money, or family living close by to help us. We are fairly normal people who raised four kids while working. Both of us had a parent who mostly stayed home to cover childcare when we were young, so we didn't have role models for a two-working-parent family.

This book contains our real-life stories about meeting goals at work and raising kids. It also contains creative solutions—also called "hacks." For technologists, the word hack has a lot of meanings. A hacker is someone who uses their expertise to overcome a problem. Although sometimes hacking is used to violate security, it is more often used by ingenious technologists with good intentions. In fact, many technology organizations host hackathons or hackfests, where technology teams collaborate intensively to solve issues. The word hack is now used by folks outside of technology for everything from dispensing pancake batter to organizing cords on a desk.

> hack: An unexpected solution to a problem;
> a work-around

My mother, Judy, was the first one to teach me about hacks. Judy always had wonderful, practical advice for me and my six siblings: If you put your bread dough on the hood of a car you took out earlier, even if it is a cool day, your bread will rise. Bourbon on gums helps teething babies. If you put on lipstick and a coat, no one can tell you are still wearing your nightgown when you take your kids to school after they missed the bus.

The truth of the matter is that none of her practical advice helped me at my first job at a small tech firm after I announced I was pregnant. My boss gave me a big smile and, in an understanding tone, said, "Once you see that baby's face, I know you won't want to come back here." He then immediately moved my projects to other people.

Granted, that was around twenty-five years ago, but challenges still exist in the workplace for anyone trying to both raise a family and stay in the stream of meaningful full-time work.

I have worked in IT for wonderful leaders at wonderful companies, and I have always been involved in women's networks. I've come to expect questions about navigating technology careers whenever I lead a workshop or discussion, but I remain surprised by the number of young people asking how to pull off having kids while thriving in their careers.

I'm of the first generation where dual-working parents became common, and much of what we navigated has become the new normal. I noticed that, as I shared ideas with my younger colleagues about what worked for our family, I was sharing both traditional ideas and hacks—unexpected ways to solve work-life balance problems. I've learned that, while using ideas and hacks is important to me, even more important is sharing them to help others save time and find positive results.

This book has short sections on particular themes. The hope is that you can pick it up for ten minutes and then return to it a day later and easily start a new section.

This book was created to capture the stories from my life juggling work, love, sanity, and practical matters. I believe that stories "stick," stay in our memories, and keep us smiling, laughing, and nodding together. I have included valuable advice I gathered both from my experiences throughout the years and from my colleagues. That said, here's my advice about advice, which also goes for the advice in this book:

Our first child Olivia had colic. One night, when we were at dinner with my parents, I paced with my fussy baby in the lobby, and a woman struck up a conversation. She could tell I was kind of frantic and offered helpful suggestions about how to hold Olivia to warm her stomach. The woman mentioned she was a nurse and worked with children. I asked if she had other advice. She laughed and said, "Only listen to the advice you like. Seriously, for every person who says, 'It's cold, that baby needs a hat,' you can walk two blocks and someone will say, 'That baby is melting in the hat and needs air.'"

She was right. We found that it worked best for us to make the decisions that felt right for our family. We had our kids play sports because it kept them healthy, but we didn't push them into elite competitive sports levels or music lessons because of our budget and our worries that it would impact our time together as a family. We had friends whose kids played instruments or were on elite sports teams, and all their kids—and ours—turned out just fine.

My point: only use the advice that helps you.

It is my hope that this book makes you laugh and that it helps you, your family, and your work thrive.

A Professional Generation with Limited Role Models

As working parents, we are problem-solving a multitude of work-life situations that our parents and some of our childless peers never dealt with.

Gallup's "State of the American Workplace 2018" notes that a key place organizations fall short is in providing "flexible working locations where you can choose to work offsite full-time." A full 35 percent of employees would change their job to have this benefit, but only 12 percent of employees say their companies offer it.

Gallup also notes that organizations have "differentiating benefits . . . that a segment of organizations offer, most employees say they would change jobs to get, and correlate most highly with employee engagement and well-being," and the top perk in this category is flextime, which allows employees to have some choice in the time of day they work. A little over half of employees would change jobs for this benefit, while 44 percent say their company offers it.

Gartner's CIO Leadership Council notes that the retention rate of women in tech is half that of men; women make up 31 percent of tech organizations. They find that 45 percent of women with children experience disruption in their career versus 24 percent of men, and that the lack of "flexible working arrangements make the dual role of mother and worker unsustainable."

These are modern issues, new to the workplace. What strikes me is that as we shift through change—more women getting degrees, more two-career families, more dads becoming involved in daily parenting life—there are limited role models to look to. Our parents had very different life experiences. We are figuring this out in real-time.

The goal of *The Parent Track* is to accelerate this generation of working parents and give pragmatic ideas for creating work-life balance. My hope is that by sharing practical work-arounds and solutions that didn't exist twenty-five years ago, working parents can thrive.

> thrive: flourish, prosper, grow vigorously, develop well, blossom

Each of us decides what it means for us to thrive. I found that for me to grow vigorously in my work with good compensation and interesting work and challenges and to flourish as a parent raising kids who also thrive, I needed some new shortcuts and strategies.

Many studies find that the decision to have a family can cause stalls in career. Equally, you can feel yourself stall as a parent when your work overwhelms your life. When we do the minimum to hold steady, we are merely surviving.

Thriving is possible. You can progress in your career and do well while raising a happy and strong family, finding happiness and progress in both raising a family and in work.

My Work-Life Story

My start in tech was working for a consulting company in Chicago. I was hired because I had an English minor, and they needed help writing project proposals. The week I started, the first Intel processor–based network server was released, which initiated a new age of computing.

From the start, I was fascinated and learned quickly. I asked questions about how we designed networks, and when projects frequently hit crises, I recognized and resolved design problems and uncovered the root causes of challenges. I pitched my leadership team on a new role, suggesting that I could reduce problems in projects by organizing them at the start. At the time, I was the only woman on the team. A group of the guys I worked closely with was nicknamed "The Colossals." I still have a photo of me, nine months pregnant, comparing bellies with these imposing fellows.

This company was a small, private consulting firm where I learned how to estimate complex projects and the intricacies of technical foundations. I rescued other projects that were in trouble, defined our standards for work, and trained others to do what I did. This was my first job where I was a parent, and I started to develop survival skills for balancing my new responsibilities at home. New technologies were emerging that made remote work possible, and my terrific leadership team supported me as their first test case.

From there, I joined Volkswagen/Audi and stood up the first project management organization for the infrastructure team—which included data centers, networking, and basically every other team that didn't develop software. The infrastructure team had trouble getting funding approved because they were unable to quantify their work and progress. Within months I added just enough structure to keep us quickly completing work and to earn the CIO's trust (and funding). VW had an amazing management training program, and there I learned about myself and leading others. I was given an effective toolbox of leadership skills to manage teams, which I still use today. At VW, I developed a flex-hours model that supported my long commute and parenting responsibilities while leading a team for the first time.

When I went to Dell EMC, that leadership toolbox was critical. I was given the worst-performing team in North America for professional services. Our team ranked at the bottom of ratings for projects finishing on time and meeting budget requirements, customer satisfaction, and quality targets. I used every management skill VW taught me. I rebalanced the work over my sixteen-person team, aligned work to strengths, set goals differently, and changed the ways we measured progress. After eighteen months, the team advanced to the middle of the pack, and shortly thereafter we were ranked at the top. Today, that team continues to thrive. At Dell, I honed my efficiency so I could manage growing kids and their more complex schedules.

After my tenure at Dell, I went to McDonald's. There, I worked at a scale I hadn't before, managing the North American IT budget that supported nearly fifteen thousand locations, leading Agile software development teams, doing strategic roadmap planning for multiple years, and most importantly, learning to thrive and work with a peer team of senior leaders. McDonald's had an exceptional leadership development program at the time, and it helped me explore the needs of managing very large teams. I learned about cross-team collaboration, communication styles, and effectiveness in small and large settings, and I left McDonald's with a clearer perspective of what is needed from a leader when teams and responsibilities are complex. I worked around the changing needs of my growing kids and the pressures on leaders to be part of evening events.

At Brookfield, I led the transition to Agile software

development, led large-scale technical strategy, established our governance and measurement, and built practices leveraged for some of our global divisions. I created our talent pipeline development, am active in Chicago-based women in technology networks, and keep track of the people I help progress across the career lattice or up the career ladder. This matters deeply to me; I want to help turn the tide of women who have been leaving technology and help make progress against the existing gender pay gap.

In my career, each of my roles built on the last and I progressed in responsibility and compensation.

I did all of this while parenting four children born in seven years. If I have learned nothing else, I have learned this: parenting is a grand experiment. It often seems like you don't know if you're doing parenting "right" until your children are older—graduated, doing work they love, choosing good partners, and building communities of friends who bring them joy. By that measurement, we have achieved success in parenthood as well as in work.

When I look back, here's what I recognize: My husband and I both work, and we both parent. Not only did we survive, we thrived.

Chapter 1

BE EARLY,
BE EXCELLENT

I waited tables during high school and college to cover expenses, and I learned my primary work lesson there: be early, be excellent.

Because I worked hard, showed up before my shift, paid attention to details, pitched in with my coworkers, and was responsive to customers, my tips were high and so was my manager's opinion of me. Over time, I got the best shifts, and if I needed some time off, it was granted easily. That same pattern followed when I got my first job in tech—but instead of dinner, I was delivering project plans and budgets.

I never asked for flexibility going in. I established myself as reliable and a top performer first. My bosses learned they could count on me and that my work was excellent. Because I built a reputation of excellence, I felt comfortable asking them for a flexible working arrangement, in which I worked remotely some days and on other days worked at the office for anywhere between four and twelve hours. In the seven years in which I had my four children, my husband and I went from being individual contributors to leading larger teams, having more responsibility, and delivering stronger results.

As a working parent, your instinct might be to assume that a flexible work schedule is out of the question. Perhaps you feel like you have to choose between giving more time to your family but being overlooked for a promotion and working long hours but missing time with your family. My question for you is, Can you earn your way to a flexible schedule? Are there ways to demonstrate to your team and colleagues that, whether you're in the office or not, you're responsive, reachable, and adding consistent value? The more your team trusts you, the better able you are to ask for concessions.

My hack: start with being early and doing good work.

BEING EARLY

You have learned that performance and productivity are the keys to excelling in your role. In truth, there is more to it than that. As a busy parent, you have to add discipline and planning to your work skills so you can deliver early.

Benefits of Being Early

Being early is important from three different dimensions:

You build a brand of personal reliability. Likely, you have had a moment where you worked for hours on a project, and when you presented it, someone said something to the effect of, "Oh, we didn't need a full go-live schedule with all the tasks. We just need an agenda for a go-live meeting." When you take work in progress to a team, a boss, or a business partner early, two things happen: you gain time to adjust if needed, and you reinforce your reputation as a thorough and prepared person who is not vulnerable to unforeseen delays.

You can recover if something goes wrong. When my kids were three, two, and six months, they passed around a cold. One would get a low-grade fever for a few days, then get better, then a sibling would get it. We did all the right things—healthy foods, humidifiers, fever management. This started in November, and every week some combination of the three kids was sick.

I fell behind. No holiday cards were done, and I hadn't shopped for holiday gifts. I was just keeping up with work and the little patients. On December 23, when we woke, the two-year-old's cough sounded very different, and we (all five of us) went through the snow to the doctor's office. The two-year-old had double pneumonia, and her sisters had bronchitis. The doctor said if it wasn't so close to Christmas, he would put her in the hospital— but if we promised to bring her back on Christmas Eve, he would give her antibiotic injections and allow her to stay home. He gave her the first round of shots and sent us home with orders to return the next day with a suitcase, just in case she hadn't improved and needed to go straight to the hospital.

When we returned to see the doctor, her lungs had improved. She got another round of shots, and we went home. By then, it was noon on Christmas

Eve. That meant no cards, no gifts for extended family, and no travel home to see our parents.

For the following twenty years, I did my holiday cards in November. It's a little extreme, but doing cards early gives me room to recover if something else in my schedule goes awry.

I do the same thing at work. I take an early train on big days, show up for important meetings early, and test my laptop and projection connections in rooms I am presenting in before the meeting starts. I have only needed this extra time a handful of moments in my career, but I have needed it.

It's a natural filter to prioritize what matters most. When you work to deliver a project early or fast-track a task, you automatically uncover what is crucial and what is nonessential. You consider things you might have missed, like, Does the presentation definitely need animation? Do you need the full data set to show the solution or just the leading indicators?

As they say, perfect is the enemy of good. I have found that when I work to have things prepared early, it is hard to be perfect. Instead, I can focus on making things good—which is usually what was needed from the start.

Sunday Prep

A key part of my strategy of being early is working for a few hours every Sunday afternoon so that I can go into the workweek prepared.

Yes, Sunday is the weekend. But it is also the day before a week in which you need to be at least as good, if not better, than your peers. Thirty minutes on a Sunday to set your plan and review your commitments for the week is worth hours of lost time. This is what I am looking for as I go over my calendar on Sundays:

- What are the most critical things that need to go well this week, and do I have what I need for them? This might include a meeting space or pre-meetings with others to confirm they are ready to present, have data to make decisions on, and are committed.

- Do I clearly understand which home responsibilities I am covering and which Jim is covering, and does my calendar reflect those? (For example: Have I marked in my calendar that I am working elsewhere on days that I work remote? Have I blocked out a doctor's appointment on my schedule?)

- Are there any conflicts that I can move?

- Are there any unnecessary meetings that I can move?

- Are there any meetings that I can shorten?

- Are there any meetings I will be remote for that need to have dial-ins added?

- Are there any big tasks that need prep time and, if so, should I block time out on the calendar for that preparation?

- Have the people I need most in meetings or workshops agreed to attend?

- Do I see any "land mines"—meetings that are likely to go long or go badly—that might need additional support?

- Do I have time planned to get my work done that isn't tied to a calendar event (like analyzing results, writing discussion documents, or preparing status updates)?

Solving these on Sundays helps keep me from being caught by surprise during the week. If there is something I have forgotten, this is my reminder time, and I have Sunday night or early Monday morning to recover.

In tech, progress means that things are constantly changing—so each week always has adjustments. It feels powerful to know what is coming in the next few days and to have a plan for it.

Never Miss a Deadline

There will always be work that can't be done as planned on time, for many reasons. But if you start on projects immediately, you can recognize early on if the deadline isn't feasible.

When you go to your boss on day three or day four of a ten-day work cycle, you can discuss how to adjust. This creates a trusting partnership. You also can renegotiate the content while meeting the date. When you go to your boss on day nine of ten to say you will miss the deadline, you kill off their goodwill and trust in you.

Being early does so much for your personal brand. It affects how others see you, how you recover from unexpected delays, and how you prioritize. Sundays are an excellent time to start work early, quickly find problems, and reset.

BEING EXCELLENT

Although you can easily commit to being early, excellence—the professional quality of your work—will take practice and will also involve trying (and maybe failing at) a few different strategies.

Have you ever noticed that professors give students extensions on work when the student faithfully comes to class and gets strong grades? Have you noticed that the stars of athletic teams are often allowed to rest instead of attending every practice? When someone has excellent performance, flexibility and new opportunities are easily given.

Top performance is measured in different ways depending on one's field, but some strategies for being excellent apply to all fields.

Preparation

Being prepared sets the foundation for excellent results. Here are some proven ways to prepare.

Pre-reads. When presenting content at a meeting, send the content out in advance. It's a way to show you are prepared in advance, and it gives others a chance to review the content and be ready with contributions and questions of their own. It also elevates you and your meetings from others.

Discussion documents. When working on a complex deliverable, try to meet with your boss shortly after the assignment is given with a one-page mock-up or explanation of your thoughts and approach. It lets her see that you are working on things already and gives her a chance to suggest adjustments before you have invested too much time in the deliverable. Likewise, when leading a group to solve a problem, have a one-page discussion document so that people have something to consider and jot notes on. Perhaps it is a table of three options, a diagram of an architecture change, or a quick pro/con summary of choices; in all cases, it should summarize the problem at the top.

Aggressive calendar management. A clear sign of competence is how you manage your own time and how you manage events that impact others as well. When you look at your calendar for the week on the Friday or Sunday before that week starts, you can do all of the following:

– Clear conflicts and move things if needed.

– Confirm meetings with uncertainty (a lunch meeting set two weeks ago, a meeting with a team lead who travels a lot with no notice).

– Remind others of their prework, and send yours.

– Block time after big meetings if you are responsible for the recap, action items, or follow-up.

Preparation shows your professionalism and helps your projects start well.

Pay Attention to What Makes You Excellent

Each of us has unique talents that differentiate us from others, and those unique talents have been proven to be tied to stronger outcomes in the workplace.

Once, when I was at VW, my boss Gary called me into his office and talked about an extranet issue. We had an application that quickly verified credit so we could provide leases or loans to our dealers in the US—but when it was down, the dealer just contacted a local bank. We'd get the car sale but would lose the financing deal. Each hour the extranet was down, we lost hundreds of thousands of dollars. The issue had been going on for more than a month, and tensions were high. The software team was starting to blame one of my peers for load-balancing devices our team had installed a few weeks prior.

Gary said, "I want you to go solve it. The team is waiting for you in the large conference room."

I am sure I looked like a fish out of water. I unintelligibly said, "Uh, uh, uh." I couldn't find the words at first. "I have no software experience. I am a lot younger than the folks in the room, and I have other work going on."

Gary smiled and said, "You are going to be fine." Then he left his office to catch his flight for meetings out of state.

His office was a long walk from the conference room. I left talking to myself and muttering, "Oh my gosh, I am going to have to start over. It's a mess. I am going to have to have everyone throw all the problems and ideas up on the whiteboards—which is going to be crazy—then I guess

21

we'll have to explain the ideas, and then we'll have to figure out what to do first . . ." As I got closer to the room, the tone inside my head changed: "We'll put it on the board, we'll look for themes, and we'll set a plan."

When I got to the room, I almost lost the confidence I'd gained on the walk. The conference room seated thirty, and nearly every seat contained an angry person. I used my lack of familiarity to ask people to explain the problems they had uncovered. We had over thirty different issues. As they discussed the problems, I recognized that some of the problems appeared to be the same as others or related, and we'd combine similar issues into one. I guided the group to the most likely possible solutions to start with. I kept teams from making multiple changes concurrently (so we would know which solution fixed the problem). It took us eight days to bring the system to stability. There were ultimately nearly twenty things we adjusted.

Gary gave me a gift by pushing me into the situation. I learned three critical things:

The walk matters. That time to breathe as I walked from the far end of the building helped me collect myself and settle my heart rate. It was essential to walking into the room ready to think and help others.

I can learn in the middle of work. I didn't know about data structures, integration layers, or database calls until after that process, but I could still ask the right questions that uncovered that some issues were duplicates, and some would need to precede the others.

Tools travel. The tools I had—critical thinking, prioritization, clarity of explanation, listening, comfort in crisis—"traveled" and applied to many things, even when I was in a foreign setting.

This works for anyone: take the time to compose yourself, have faith that you can learn while you do (don't let lack of training slow you from a challenge), and know and apply your strengths. Excellence comes from the unique strengths you have that you can apply in many settings.

Five Simple Phrases for Managing Expectations

A key to being excellent is meeting people's expectations. If your boss says, "Give me a summary of how the project turned out," you might give her a comprehensive financial analysis with graphs and trends. If she instead wanted the results of help desk calls and customer satisfaction surveys, you missed giving her what she needed and expected.

Confirming and meeting expectations is critical, and when balancing family and work, this skill becomes even more important. Certain phrases are better for managing the expectations of your teams, peers, and leaders. Here are some I teach others and wish I had learned earlier:

I have a conflict. Instead of saying, "I have a pediatrician's appointment," "I have a parent-teacher conference," or "I need to get someone from soccer," I simply say, "I have a conflict. How about we meet at two instead?" Almost every time, people say yes. When you can be counted on to get excellent work done, times can usually be negotiated and there is no need to share details.

Start of business. When someone says, "I need this by Thursday," I respond, "Oh, by start of business?" If they say yes, I just bought myself time between Wednesday at five in the evening and Thursday morning at eight. In my most hectic days of child-raising, that meant I could leave at three in the afternoon, make dinner, help with homework, tuck kids in bed, and then work for two hours at night to build the deliverable someone needed.

Sounds interesting. "Sounds interesting" is an effective response to any request for which your immediate reaction is, "Are you kidding me?" It is a stall tactic that keeps things positive and encourages the speaker to give more detail while you regroup. I use this when someone suggests a large, complex initiative that I have concerns about having capacity for or getting to an excellent outcome.

I had a boss who would say we "should redesign the team" (a complex effort that could be disruptive to work already in progress). I would say, "Interesting, tell me more," and as she added more detail, it would come to light that what she actually wanted to do was add analytics capacity so we could better track progress and get early indications of trouble. That clarification uncovered that her need was something the team could do without risking other work we already had underway.

I have a hard stop. When I know I must depart from a meeting or conference at a certain time, I set an expectation with the group at the start of the day or meeting: "I have a hard stop at three." I will even ask if there are any concerns with timing. If someone needs me to stay late at the meeting, I have some time to make a call and try to get someone to help me with my next commitment.

Go ahead and book time on my calendar. When you work a flexible schedule (starting or ending at nontraditional times), work remotely (telecommuting and getting work done away from the office), or extreme-flex (doing both in an inconsistent schedule), a key part of managing others' expectations is your calendar.

In our calendaring system at work, I allow others to see my meeting titles (not the attendees or contents of the meetings, which include notes or agendas). This gives transparency to where I am and what I am working on.

When I know I will be remote, I block my calendar to show "working elsewhere" so that people know I am available and will be on the calls or web meetings. When I know I need to cover something at home (like dropping off at school or a doctor's appointment), I block the time on my calendar and mark the meeting private. I make a point to be as professional when I am remote as I am in person: I am on time for calls, focused on the discussion, available through messaging systems, and in a quiet space for discussions.

I block things far in advance. For example, when my children were in school, I would put a hold on my calendar every day from three in the afternoon to five, just in case I needed to pick up from school. Then, if Jim could cover that day, I would delete the calendar hold so people could add meetings.

The times I have had to ask someone to rebook a meeting because I have a conflict are nearly non-existent, and people are confident that they can find me and understand my workload.

These phrases set a professional tone that is critical, especially if you are able to work a different schedule than the norm.

Know Your Personal Brand

In addition to professional time, your appearance helps others see your excellence.

When I was at VW, I worked closely with our organizational development director. She helped me create professional development programs for our project managers and was an important and effective partner. She noticed that I would literally run from one meeting to another with my laptop, notebooks, files, and other gear I needed for my meetings for that day.

She thoughtfully asked me once how I thought I

appeared, and I replied, "Really busy." Then she asked me how many of my male peers I had seen running to meetings with a stack of stuff. I was surprised and replied, "None."

She asked, "Is there a chance that others look at you and perceive you as disorganized and late?" I realized how right she was, and I stopped running.

As a counter to that, a friend who worked for a consulting firm shared with me that her firm addresses walking in their employee handbook. They are directed to always walk "with a sense of purpose."

The beauty of these two pieces of advice is that there is a personal brand that you share even in the simple movement between meetings and activity. When you walk with purpose (but don't rush), dress more like leaders than staff, or remain composed, you are reinforcing your brand as an excellent and reliable contributor.

The Best Tips for Your Presentations

Tone and appearance are important. No matter what your profession, how you explain things to groups of people to get their support, approval for funding, and agreement on how to solve a challenge is essential. Your presence, composure, organization, and confidence are key parts of how people will judge your ideas.

Simply practicing is a completely underestimated strategy for public speaking. I have seen poor speakers transform into orators of merit with simple repetition.

I had volunteered to read at our church, where a normal service had fifteen hundred people in a sweeping set of rows that almost went in a circle. When I went to the training session, I sat by a tiny woman in her eighties who I had heard doing wonderful readings before. She watched as I scribbled notes about how we were supposed to enter, the timing and order of actions, and the locations to sit and stand. She could tell I was nervous and wanted to do well. She leaned over, softly tapped me on my arm, and said, "Ten times." I thought I didn't hear her, so I asked what she said. She told me that she practiced ten times, out loud, every time. I figured I would try anything, so in my bedroom at home, I used the practice book and read the piece ten times out loud.

On Sunday, when I went to the microphone, the book they had for me to read from was set in a different typeface and had different page breaks than the practice book. I started reading and lost my place fairly quickly. Muscle memory took over, and I was able to keep talking even while I was finding my spot again. I realized that the repetition had allowed me to get to a point of almost fully memorizing it, and it made it easier for me to maintain eye contact with my audience and be aware of my surroundings.

At one of my companies, the CEO was a charismatic fellow. When he spoke to large groups, he made the audience feel like he was just informally sharing thoughts with everyone. He seemed so knowledgeable and comfortable. His chief of staff later told me that he practices—including his movements, pauses, and tone—twenty or more times before each presentation.

Since then, I practice often. I find it helps me master content so I can focus on my volume, projection, and how the audience is responding. At first, my presentations sounded somewhat scripted; with more practice, they sounded conversational, credible, and compelling. Whether it's a tiny and silver-haired lady, a tall CEO, or me, practice makes a difference.

I also got helpful advice from a class on telling stories that I took as part of the leadership development program at McDonald's. Our teacher, a wonderful Broadway actor, helped us tell different stories over the course of three days. After each story, he gave us feedback around preparation, physical movement, voice projection, or the arc of the story. It was the hardest class I have ever taken, and he gave me advice that applies both in work and in parenting.

He said, "Christine, you jump into your stories. Stop. Breathe. Breathe deeply. It helps you collect yourself. In the moment when you take deep breaths, you can look at the people you are going to talk to, and it gives a sense to your audience that you are in control, though the alternative might be true. It also gives you the oxygen you need to project what you are saying and helps you start off speaking at a measured pace."

This simple advice has become a game changer for me, and I realized that speaking calmly at a measured pace adds to my credibility.

The Power of Breathing and Composure

Before I speak professionally (especially in front of very large groups) or head into big meetings, and even sometimes when I stand at the train station, I do Amy Cuddy's two-minute power pose. Cuddy, a psychologist, discovered that standing in certain postures could make you feel more powerful. The two minutes of focused posture and breathing give me a sense of peace and strength.

While breathing and composure help in public speaking, I believe they also create excellence across many activities. When I work out, I pay attention to my breathing and posture. I sometimes go into a workout class carrying the frustration of the day, but I have never left a class still carrying the weight of those feelings. When I leave a high-stakes meeting, I usually take deep breaths at my desk as I replay what is next on my schedule. When my children frustrate me, I stop, breathe in, and wait until I feel more centered before I respond. At times, I will even let someone (my children, coworkers) know that I don't think I will give my best answer in the moment and ask if I can respond later.

When you feel frustration rising, your heart racing, or your inner thoughts becoming negative, it is time to stop and breathe. When you plan to pause and breathe in and out, you give yourself a chance to gather your thoughts, settle your heart rate, change direction to what you are doing next, and deliver excellence.

Run a Strong Meeting

Speaking is a solitary act, but running a meeting is something you do for people (or, if you're bad at running meetings, it is something you do *to* people). There is nothing like a strong meeting. In those meetings, the team walks into the room needing a problem solved or a plan created. The right people are in the room, and when the meeting ends on time or early, you walk out with a solution or an approach that you didn't have before.

Here are the best ways to be a meeting superstar and run strong meetings:

Manage attendees. Only have the people you need in the meeting. Studies say the group size should never exceed eight, and most effective working teams are between three and six.

Only book the time you need. Understand what needs to get completed; if you only need twenty minutes, book twenty minutes.

Agendas. Create and share the agenda, which should include the goal of the meeting, its expected outcome, who is attending, discussion points, and any prework attendees need to complete or be familiar with.

Be early. Make sure technologies you need to project, connect, and collaborate are working.

Note the new faces. When participating in a big meeting where there are people you don't know, draw a picture of the table on your notes, and as each person introduces themselves, write their name in their location for quick reference.

Recap. At the end of the meeting, recap action items with the responsible person's name, action item, and date expected to be completed.

Send action items out quickly. The best time to send any follow-ups is while the meeting is fresh in folks' minds.

Take selective notes. I suggest not writing down everything that is said and instead only capturing decisions made or action items. Dense notes are rarely read and take time and attention.

Have a lookout. If the meeting is large, have someone help watch participants. If you are at the board or focusing on an exchange with one person, the lookout can watch others to see if the group reflects concern or confusion. Your lookout can ask for a quick pause and bring other questions or voices into the discussion that you as the facilitator might have missed.

Diversify your approach. Get to know facilitation methods that work for introverts and extroverts, and use both.

Meetings are the heart of business work, whether to make decisions, work as a group, update leadership, inform, or lead organizations through change. When people complain about meetings, they are complaining about the bad ones. I believe that running good meetings is the single best thing you can do to improve your professional career. When you run effective meetings, you positively impact not only your productivity but the productivity of all who meet with you.

Hack Recap: Be Early, Be Excellent

The foundational component of your career will be your performance. You need your reputation to be strong so that you are afforded flexibility to raise your family, whether it is flextime, remote work, or sensitivity about non-office hours. Being early and excellent is an effective path to this goal and includes everything we've discussed:

- Deliver ahead of schedule

- For critical meetings, arrive early

- Aim for good (and on time), not perfect

- Consider working on Sundays to plan parenting responsibilities as well as lining up the workweek

- Be prepared (with pre-reads, discussion documents, and a well-planned schedule)

- Know your own strengths so you can use them as often as possible

- Set expectations by employing effective phrases like "I have a conflict" or "by start of business"

- Understand your personal brand—how you appear to others and how that influences their perceptions of your quality of work

- Practice your speeches, and mind your breathing

- Run great meetings

Chapter 2

SET AND TRACK YOUR GOALS

You are off to a great start. You are early. You are excellent. You are seeing progress in your work and your life. A key part of building on this base is setting goals and objectives around both work and life.

When Kate was born, one of her sisters was three years old and the other was eighteen months old. Days blended together, and there would be weeks when I felt like I had accomplished nothing. My spirits would get low.

When I started defining and tracking my goals, my spirits rose significantly because I realized how much I was getting done. I also saw nonessential items slip their way onto my lists, recognized that they weren't actually important, and removed them. Goal setting helps quantify progress and build self-awareness around how terrific you actually are even when you are too tired to recognize it.

I changed how I set goals in three ways:

WEEKLY

Each week I set goals. I look at the meetings and work ahead and define things I need to accomplish for work; I figure out which days I can exercise and what I plan to do;

and I add personal goals. At the start of the week, it looks like this:

Personal	Neighborhood cards with Jim
	Send Mom a birthday card
	Help girls find rocks for project
Exercise	Monday: run
	Wednesday: early class
	Friday: run
Work	Successful review with architects
	Draft of plan for migration
	Projected headcount for team redesign
	Budget audit for Q3 spend

At the end of each week, I go back through the list. I add a dot where things were completed and a dash where something needs to move to the next week. At the bottom, I write things I am grateful for. The things I am grateful for can be small, like one of the kids getting all the bonus spelling words right, a recipe turning out, or my boss loving a deliverable.

These two acts of checking off what I have done and noting what I am grateful for have helped me see the progress I am making despite the rapid pace and full days. Now, each week has an accounting of progress, and the exercise of summarizing blessings helps me slow down and feel gratitude. It provides an infusion of confidence and positive feelings before a new week starts.

YEARLY

Each year, I set goals. While I set stretch goals—targets that are difficult or potentially uncomfortable to achieve—I am also realistic. For example, I am not going to take a full course load for my master's program and work full-time with three young children. Maybe, though, I can apply and get in, or take a class sometime during the year. That process of thinking about what can realistically be done is helpful. I use a model that includes focus on all parts of life, and it helps me realize when I am overlooking something. An adapted example is on the following page.

Some simple, smaller goals I have set for my own professional development include writing blogs to build toward writing a book and going to an open-mic night to give five-minute lightning talks so I can work on content for larger talks. These smaller steps can fit into a busy life and give you confidence even when you are swamped with work and caring for others. These smaller steps move you toward where you want to be.

MULTIYEAR

Sometimes, it seemed like Jim and I were getting raises and promotions but not getting ahead. To prepare for future financial commitments, I created a model to look at child-care costs and predict expenses for college. The timeline showed the ages of my kids by year and what the tuition

Parenting
– T—reading, patience
– N—math, persistence
– Library weekly
– Leave phone in car
when they are awake

Love
– Hug
– Low tech dates
– Leave love notes

2020

Learning/Professional
– Writing—publish 3 articles
– Apply an innovative strategy
from a conference
– Personal technology
– Speak at annual conference

Finances
– Short term
household gains
– Complete 2020 whole,
retire medical debt

Work
– Agile adoption success
– Innovation
– Strengths oriented strategy
for self and team
– Journal about meaning and
soft accomplishments
– Set goals around meaning

Health
– Class 3-4x week
– Hydrate
– Sleep
– Core

Fun
– Trip in March
– Rent an apartment in
Chicago
– Laugh
– Something new, social
once a month

load would be. We included when cars would be paid off, when a medical debt would be retired, and other financial variables. We could see how our earning patterns needed to adapt to support our family's financial plan. This model was borne out of a lot of sacrifice and frustration, and it helped us see two things: challenges before they hit (like three children in college simultaneously), and where the "light in the tunnel" was—when we would feel relief.

If you look at the example on the next page for a family with two young children, the hard years are going to be 2021–2023 and 2030–2035. However, there will be less pressure in 2026 and 2027; those would be peak savings years to get ready for expensive years ahead.

Six-Month Resets

A key part of setting goals was to regroup as a couple and make sure things were working well. Jim and I would do this regroup roughly every six months. We'd go out, take a notebook, and talk about how things were going. Usually we sat in a pub close to our house, sometimes with a laptop, sometimes just with paper.

At one point when we regrouped, he was working on some large projects in China and needed to travel for a few weeks at a time. I scaled back my work so I could cover all the child pickups and drop-offs. Another time, I took a job that had expectations of after-hours meetings and planning sessions, so he curbed his travel so he could cover dinners in case I was out late.

Each time one of us started a new job, the other would make sure they could cover home responsibilities. That

	2019	2020	2021	2022	2023	2024	2025	2026	2027	2028	2029	2030	2031	2032	2033	2034	2035
T's Age	2	3	4	5	6	7	8	9	10	11	12	13	14	15	16	17	18
N's Age	5	6	7	8	9	10	11	12	13	14	15	16	17	18	19	20	21
Nanny	■	■	■														
Sitters				■	■	■	■	■	■	■	■						
Car 1	■	■	■	■	■												
Car 2						■	■	■	■	■	■	■					
Car 3												■	■	■	■		
HS Tuition T													■	■	■	■	
HS Tuition N										■	■	■	■				
College Tuition T																	■
College Tuition N														■	■	■	■

way, the person with the new job could invest the time to be a top performer in the new organization and, in time, earn flexibility and support.

We made these decisions together. We were both faced with relocation options at different times, and we did the math on what the cost would be to establish a new base—that one of us would need to be out of work for a while to set up all the systems we needed to thrive: childcare, a pediatrician, a barber, groceries, a new soccer league, and a new school, to name a few. At times, we each took jobs with pay cuts to get flexibility, and we each took big raises with new opportunities. We had a rule that only one of us could be in crisis at a time, and for the most part, we succeeded in sticking to it.

There were other factors beyond our careers that we considered in our decisions. Sometimes we would talk about how the kids were missing the parent who was working long hours, or how one of our children was going through a challenge.

When our third daughter Kate was born, she seemed to struggle to catch her breath. By her fourth day, she was turning blue and gasping. We raced to the hospital and I told her wonderful lies—that she was my favorite, that she was so clearly smarter than her sisters, and so on. If she died in my arms, I wanted the last thing she heard to be me loving her, not me telling her dad to run red lights. I rushed into the ER with her and got a semi-condescending look from a nurse who said, "First baby?" When I replied that she was my third, the nurse raced me back to a doctor. Kate had surgery before she was a week old and stayed in intensive care. She had surgery again at four weeks old and again at eleven months. Each time, we didn't want to leave her alone in the hospital. We had no relatives who lived nearby, just our babysitter, so one of us would stay at home with the eighteen-month-old and the three-year-old. During the day, the sitter would come and the parent at home would work remotely like normal. The parent at the hospital would work on a laptop while Kate slept.

We switched off every day, taking turns sleeping on the floor of the hospital room. Kate was only ever alone for the amount of time it took one parent to go down to the lobby and meet the car with her other parent and her sisters.

It was intense. Each of us had to take some time off, but we kept working enough to keep our projects going. This model of looking ahead and making decisions to split up the time and the responsibilities was key to us for surviving that time.

Empty-Nest Goals

Goals at all stages are important. I was at a neighborhood gathering one night when two friends started crying about how they sent their youngest off to college. I noticed my friend Nancy wasn't crying, even though her youngest was headed off too. I asked her why she wasn't upset, and she replied, "Christine, I believe that if you have done everything right as a parent—you didn't miss a parent-teacher conference, you stayed up to make sure they were home on time, you went to games, you knew their friends—two things happen: One, your children are ready. And two, you are tired." We both laughed and laughed.

Nancy also shared with me that she and her husband

were afraid that the transition to having free time would be hard. During the months before their youngest left, they went on dates on Friday nights and took a notebook in which they wrote things that they always wanted to do but hadn't because their kids were around and they were busy. Their list included remodeling a bathroom themselves and taking a sailing trip with friends. Now, their bathroom is beautiful and the sailing trip has become an annual event.

Jim and I took their idea. We had our kids early and haven't had a chance to travel much. We have a goal to do something different at least once a month. We take shorter trips to see our kids and do things we wished we could have done more. One weekend, we hiked through canyons in a state park and then stopped at an architectural museum on the way home. We are trying to figure out where we want to live in the future, so we are staying in places and cities for weekends at a time to get a sense for what fits for us.

Maybe most importantly, we set goals for how we want to stay connected with our grown-up kids. We plan trips to see them, and both of us try to connect with all four of them every week.

In all the phases of raising children, we continued to talk about what we want to do as parents, in our jobs, and with each other. The goals change, but the process endures.

For our work, our goals include investigating new models of working for the last parts of our careers, like consulting and relocation, and trying things we have always had on our personal bucket lists.

Hack Recap: Goal Setting

Writing down goals helps set a plan. And, more importantly, when you look back at your progress, you can count up small wins and see how far you have come, even if you feel tired or overwhelmed. Goals (and reviewing progress) are an effective way to focus on the present with awareness of long-term impacts, and keep your spirits up even in busy times. Favorite hacks include:

- Weekly goals with end-of-week reviews for professional and personal goals and a quick recap of blessings

- Yearly goals about all facets of your life for a chance to stop and consider what is most important in the coming months

- Multiyear plans for finances, career transitions, and larger issues like childcare and education needs

- Six-month resets with your partners for adjustments based on what is working and not working for your family

- Empty-nest goals to make the transition between two very different periods of life

Chapter 3

ADOPT AN EXTREME EFFICIENCY MINDSET AT WORK

You are early. You are excellent. You have goals and plans. The problem is that kids are not efficient.

There are studies and friends who will note that having kids usually isn't good for your career. That is the truth. Just like the goals of becoming a world-class runner and of rapidly developing your business career are at odds with each other, having a family can sometimes interfere with thriving at work. The truth is that raising children takes time, and that time spent raising your kids will undoubtedly impact your work.

No more last-minute working sessions over dinner. No more arriving at the office at six every morning to get a jump on the day. You may turn down promotions because they require relocation and your child would have to leave the sports team they captain, change nannies, disrupt a critical school year, or leave a medical specialist you rely on.

Also, little things happen. Every day. I remember being ready to walk out the door for a big meeting and hugging my kids goodbye when the six-month-old burped down the front of my dark suit. I had to sprint up the stairs to change every piece of clothing before racing out the door.

There were times that I needed four hours of focused work time to get something done and was counting on one of the kids to get to sleep or for my husband to get home, but instead the baby stayed up or his flight was canceled. I had to scramble in the early days, and sometimes things were left unfinished. I learned to adapt to things not going as I had hoped. These pressures, coupled with scrambling to get work done, had the unintended consequence of helping me become efficient at an extreme level.

Efficiency Habits Are Good for Your Career

When I was young, my role model for professional work was my father. He worked very hard for long hours. Once, I asked him if he was always ambitious. He replied cheerfully: "I got more ambitious with each one of you." Punch line: there were seven of us. Yes, he was one of the hardest-working men I knew. Because of this, we saw him mostly on weekends and late in the evenings.

Unlike my father, I had the benefit of using and working in technology. Tech gave me ways to be connected to information and people regardless of my location or the time of day. My dad didn't have those options to help his efficiency.

I worked aggressively smart (and long—but also remotely and with flexible hours). The skill I developed most was vigilant prioritization. Nothing motivated me to figure out the fastest way to solve a problem more than a car-line pickup deadline at school. Nothing motivated me more to structure meetings efficiently than needing every minute of my face time in the office. I didn't linger over nonessential messages, articles, or distractions.

The payoff was four little ones at the kitchen table doing homework while we made dinner and talked about toads, great books, science experiments, and lost gloves. I was all-in at the office, and I was all-in while in the kitchen cooking, and on the couch reading books, and on the floor working puzzles.

To be completely honest, I was not all-in in every aspect of my life. When it came to my fitness, keeping up with friends, finishing the books for book club, keeping the house clean, and heaven knows what else, many things went undone. But, every day, I flexed my decision-making muscle and prioritized where and how to invest my time. It made me better at being a parent, a partner, and part of a professional team. It made my projects impactful and profitable, and I learned a lot about toads from those conversations with my kids.

FILTER WORK A.K.A. LET THE PLANTS DIE

One of the specific ways I became more efficient was in solving the challenge of finding time to get everything done. Learning how to filter work and understand what is truly necessary is a key skill to develop.

"Oh crap, I'm watering the plants." That was how Emily started our call the other day. Emily is a mentee of mine and the youngest employee on her team. She had been listening to *Women at Work* (a well-regarded podcast out of the Harvard Business Review). The particular podcast was about women and people of color being assigned or volunteering for "non-promotable" work like taking notes, watering office plants, or ordering lunch. As she listened to the podcast, she recognized that, though she was a peer in terms of education and contribution to her team, over time there was an assumption that she would take on certain tasks. Her desk was by the door, so people assumed she should receive and send packages and welcome visitors— but mostly, everyone assumed she would water the plants.

This, combined with her lack of progress to more complicated work, demoralized her. She talked (maybe ranted a bit) and I listened. I said, "Emily, you have to let the plants die." She laughed, and we talked seriously about how to start to turn the tide. We talked about a solution that included two things in a statement—a gentle "no" or delay, and a reinforcement of her work.

If someone asked her to mail a package, she could reply, "I should have some time tomorrow; today I need to get this analysis done for the board." If someone asked her to plan the happy hour, she could reply, "I really wish I could, but I have a meeting with the team to solve the setback from Tuesday." If asked why the plants were dying, she could reply, "Oh gosh, feel free to water them. I've been heads-down on the new interface work."

With each interaction, she keeps her professional relationships strong and starts to build a new narrative: she is too busy with critical project work to do nonessential tasks. It's a way to reinforce who she is on the team—a bright person trusted with executive communications, crisis management, and key emerging work.

She was recently promoted, and yes, plants were harmed in the process.

Organize Your Daily Work

Emily learned how to focus on key tasks and manage her personal brand by focusing on meaningful work. Another key practice is to track your meaningful work daily.

Everyone who has worked with me notices that I carry a notebook with me everywhere I go. Mine is divided into sections:

Early. At the top of the page, I write tasks that were done before the business day started.

Face-to-face/office. Meetings go down the right side, in order of occurrence, tasks down the left side.

Thinking tasks. These can be done on the train or moved to a work-remote day.

Personal. Things I need to keep track of, like rescheduling a doctor appointment.

Things to talk to my boss about. These go in the back of the notebook. I collect questions and updates, so when I meet with her I can easily debrief a week.

Analysis for another day. This also goes in the back of the notebook. These things need silence and focused thought. I keep a running list and save these analytic tasks for days when I work remote.

At a glance, I can see what to do when I have a small break between working sessions with my teams.

A quick plug for the manual notebook: I read a study by Mueller and Oppenheimer that compared handwritten notes to notes on a laptop, and the results resonated with me. Overall, they found that taking notes by hand seemed to lead to different cognitive processing. Since writing by hand is slower and more cumbersome, students couldn't capture every word. Instead, they were summarizing and digesting the essence of the information. The researchers hypothesized that deep cognitive processes were part of handwriting notes. I find that to be the case for me. The placement of my notes—along with whether I use capitals, arrows, or underlining to highlight—helps me quickly organize information. The physical notebook helps me work through priorities and classify work. A good friend uses a list app, and her multiple categories seem to solve the same issues. It is purely preference.

Here are the key questions to ask yourself: Before the day starts, have you done the work of prioritizing? Do you have mechanisms to catch emerging and unexpected work that occurs during the day?

FOUR SECRETS TO OPTIMIZING YOUR MINUTES

Keeping track of work, whether in a notebook or by some other means, is critical. The second step is to optimize your time to complete work. Every minute of the workday is precious, especially for work-life balance. These are some of my favorite strategies for optimizing those minutes.

Face-to-Face Time

While there are many technologies to help us connect with each other virtually, face-to-face time remains critical to working well with teams.

One of my mentors once said, "It is impossible to sustain anger when you are face-to-face. It is easy when you are sitting in your office writing emails but much harder when you look someone in the eye and need to work through something." When I am in the office, time is optimized for face-to-face interaction. I normally meet with people through lunch and set up meetings all day.

I used to do solitary work at the office, but I realized that I got that work done faster when I was in my home work space. Moving solitary work to work-remote days also helped me focus on others and collaborate when I was in the office.

When I am in a situation where I am working remotely full-time and unable to go to the office to meet others, I use video calling or conferencing to make connections and call folks to talk on the phone if video options aren't available.

The 20/45 Rule

Meetings can be a wasteful use of time. I use the 20/45 rule: meetings that would normally be thirty minutes, I try to complete in twenty; meetings that would normally be an hour, I try to complete in forty-five. That earns me appreciation from the folks who attend my meetings, gives me time to quickly write up notes or actions, and offers a chance for everyone to reset before the next meeting.

Use Commuting Time Wisely

In Chicago, long commutes are the norm. Mine is two hours a day on the train, plus additional time driving to and from the station. Those two-plus hours add up, and in that time, I get work done. When I commute via car, I set up conference calls via hands-free for the duration of the ride or use the time to catch up with family. When I commute via train, I do solitary work on my device. Because of the productive nature of the time, I count these as working hours.

Don't "Admire Your Walls"

A key part of being efficient is not wasting time on things you can't change or on overthinking your barriers. Have you ever known someone who comes up against a challenge—a challenge that is so complicated that it's like their progress is blocked by a big wall—and who, instead of tackling the problem, sits back and admires it?

Think of the college student who says, "I'm never going to finish my final assignment. This paper is impossible to write. I have forty sources, and my thesis statement isn't coming together, and the data doesn't support my conclusion, and I am starting to feel sick, and did you know this professor gets terrible ratings because this paper is too hard, and my seat at the library that I usually sit in was occupied . . ." They are admiring the wall, letting you know how big and insurmountable their barrier is while, at the same time, doing nothing to get the assignment completed.

Another way I think about it is like this: if a team is trapped in a cave with a limited oxygen supply, complaining and worrying only wastes their precious resources.

Unless the comments help the team find their way out, words without purpose just eat up oxygen.

If you were a wall admirer before, having children should help you break the habit of focusing on the barriers you encounter. Don't lose time worrying about a meeting you were late to. You were late, it happened, don't do it again. Don't worry about having someone help you with childcare when you stayed late; stuff happens, just try not to make a habit of it. When something goes differently than you expected, the faster you turn your thoughts to solutions, the more time you have for the things you care about.

Advantages of Working Fast

In addition to focusing on possibilities instead of barriers to solutions, a key part of efficiency is quickly confirming you are on track. These are some of my favorite solutions:

Fast Drafts

When you are working on an assignment, building an incomplete but good draft fast gives your boss, team, or client something to react to. They can then refine what they need and you can complete the work with confirmation that you are heading in the right direction.

Imagine your manager asks you for next year's budget in two weeks, and they want you to change the distribution of costs based on a model. Instead of delivering the full model in two weeks, start by giving them a partial solution in a day or two, with some of the lines completed. This allows the two of you to meet and verify that you are building the budget correctly.

If a coworker asks you for a presentation for an executive group in a week and gives you some direction about needing to bring the group to a decision, give them an outline or a rough mockup of slides that same day and have a brief discussion on the order of the slides, the number, and what each slide may have on it. Then incorporate the adjustments they suggest.

Some people have asked me if this looks like an inability to run with work independently or if it suggests a need for validation. What's important is how you present your work in progress. If you frame it by saying, "I know this is important, so I got right to work on it, and I want to confirm I am taking this in the direction you had in mind," then you come across as taking ownership of the process, being responsive, and being strategic.

If you finish the project without feedback, you might end up building a perfect tool that goes unused or needs to be reworked with little time to respond.

Discussion Documents

A related solution I learned from one of my favorite mentors at Dell EMC is the concept of "discussion documents." This is a single page of insight prepared in advance of a meeting with a boss or a client. The goal is to have something to hand them that supports the discussion and any decision that needs to be made.

Discussion documents that focus on problem-solving summarize the issue—perhaps with a simple diagram or an initial diagnosis. Team-expansion discussion documents might include a current summary of team members and roles and a projected changed summary. Design-decision discussion documents might include three options being considered with pros and cons.

Discussion documents give people in the room something to jot notes on and refer to during the conversation. Just as important, the discussion document forces the author to have their thoughts together before the meeting.

The advantage of a discussion document is that it is designed to guide a conversation. The goal of the conversation is to gain a sense of whether an effort should even begin, and if so what direction it should take. A discussion document brings others into your thought process.

Rapid Meeting Notes

Another way you can help others be efficient is by sending out meeting notes within hours of the meeting. Everyone still has a fresh recall of content and can suggest adjustments and improvements. Mistakes on the writer's part are usually forgiven because of the quick turnaround. Had the notes taken a week, people might think, "Gosh, he had a whole week to get these right"; when notes come out immediately, people tend to think, "Ah, quick turnaround— just missed this one thing." Bullets, simple formatting, and consistent, quick responses show that the meeting facilitator is on top of details and managing time and wants to help others review when everyone is still able to recall the meeting's content.

This practice builds efficiency by allowing you to respond with a limited amount of effort in a way that optimizes your time (short format) and your team's time (receiving notes when their minds are still fresh from discussing the content).

Dress for Success in Five Minutes or Less

Many of these last suggestions have been about working with others. One simple and personal way you can be inefficient is in dressing for the day. Have you ever stood in your closet, glaring at your clothes and watching the minutes tick by while you try to figure out what to wear?

When I was growing up, there was a clothing line for children called "Garanimals." Its premise was that if you found a shirt with a giraffe on the tag, any pants with a giraffe tag on them would match. It was a fail-proof matching system. My closet looks like a grown-up Garanimals shop. I wear simple pieces in solid grays, blacks, and blues that can be switched around. I get dressed quickly, I have a consistent look, and I don't have to worry about whether something is appropriate or in fashion. This isn't for everyone, but it saves me a lot of time.

INEFFICIENCY CAN RECHARGE YOU

It might seem odd that, in this chapter on efficiency, there is a section about being inefficient, but stick with me. I have a good reason. Sometimes, disconnecting from the plan can help you break through a mental block or find a solution to a problem.

One summer evening, shortly after the school summer break started, life was going as normal. My youngest was in high spirits because his sisters were home during the day. I'd had a challenging day; I had been working on a network design for a while, and it was going more slowly than I'd expected. Jim was on the road, and we had just finished baths. Everyone put on pajamas, then immediately put on their Harry Potter robes from Halloween the year before and started playing as if they attended Hogwarts School of Witchcraft and Wizardry. Outside, the sun was starting to set.

Normally, during the school year, the kids would have gone to bed and I would have returned to my laptop to press on through my remaining work. Instead, I suggested we walk down to the park. An outing in the growing dark was unusual and exciting.

I remember walking down the sidewalk with four little wizards with their robes and wands in front of me. They ran around the field in the park, chasing lightning bugs and casting spells. As I sat on a bench and let their games unfold, my worries from the day slipped away into the corners of the night. I found peace in the cool night air and the joyous shouts of my kids running around in the increasing darkness.

The peace and break renewed me, and later that night I solved problems that had seemed unsolvable before four wizards took me on a walk. So, every now and then, set efficiency aside, enjoy the fireflies, and see if it helps you solve problems.

HACK RECAP: EFFICIENCY AT WORK

If you are trying to optimize your work time to free minutes and hours for family, each minute matters. Ways you can get the most out of work time include the following:

– Filter work: focus on the most important things instead of watering plants or other noncritical tasks

- Find a mechanism to consistently track your work

- Optimize the time you are in the office
    - Try to schedule as many meetings face-to-face as possible
    - Consider the 20/45 meeting time guideline
    - Use commuting time to get things done

- Don't lose time complaining or admiring the walls you bump up against

- Work fast—send early drafts, discussion documents before full documents, and meetings notes to build in time for people to respond and for you to adjust

- Simplify your professional dress

- Consider being inefficient to regain balance, joy, and productivity

Chapter 4

ADOPT AN EXTREME EFFICIENCY MINDSET AT HOME

You have everything optimized at work. Now let's talk about hacks for home that can solve the challenges that happen in almost every family. These hacks helped us find more peace and time at home.

FREE-RANGE FEEDING FOR CHILDREN

When I was growing up, dinner was only when my dad got home from work, and there was no snacking between meals. I remember coming to the table so hungry and then eating as fast as I could. (Six siblings can motivate you to get food while it was still left.) It was only when I got older that I learned to eat when I was hungry, which didn't always line up to scheduled meals.

We wanted to raise our children to have healthy eating habits from the beginning, and we recognized early on that it was hard to cook and plan mealtimes with a menu that worked well for family members on different schedules. We knew that traditional mealtimes and rules about eating between meals wouldn't work for us.

The strategy we came up with was free-range feeding, so our kids could eat whenever they were hungry. We put healthy food within their reach on pantry shelves and in the refrigerator. We made dinner at night, and if they wanted to eat it, that was fine. If they didn't, they could get cheese, yogurt, or fruit. They ate what we made about 90 percent of the time. Jim and I cooked foods we liked and ended up with kids who ate salmon, asparagus, and other foods children often turn their noses up to.

We gave up some of our favorite cheating foods, but that was okay. When there aren't unhealthy things in the house, there aren't arguments about food. When hungry kids can easily reach food, there isn't stress about mealtimes.

We had talks with our kids about protein and what vitamins were in different fruits and vegetables. I did have one child who ate hot dogs straight for three months, and we were so worried that we asked the pediatrician about it. He laughed and said this phase would end soon, and he was right.

An extension of free-range feeding was to post a grocery list on the refrigerator. As the kids got older, we made a rule that if you ate the last of anything, you added that item to the list. If you had something you were in the mood for, you put it on the list and whoever did the grocery shopping would pick the items up.

Three of our children are primarily vegetarians (though they eat some fish). The oldest took an ethics class in seventh grade and learned about the food chain and treatment of animals. I mention this because I think a lot of children (if they aren't vegetarians already) try this diet at one point. We adjusted the free-range model to include responsibilities for vegetarians. We expected they would make deliberate decisions to incorporate protein (in our case, eggs, cheese, and fish, which they added later), and they would continue to eat healthy foods. I tried to incorporate a vegetarian protein into every meal, but if I couldn't, I expected them to figure it out. Also, if they ever had medical tests indicating issues, we would revisit the decision to be vegetarians. Thankfully, that never happened.

I now usually have two pans going on the stove—one for cacciatore with chicken and the other with just sauce. I make lasagna in two pans, one without meat. We have a good number of meals with no meat at all, just some version of black beans or tofu. And it works well. They have introduced me to new foods, and we are all healthier.

HACKS FOR RAISING MULTIPLE SMALL CHILDREN

Figuring out how to feed our kids in a healthy way helped us gain efficiency, but we underestimated the challenge of having multiple small children at the same time. One of the best sources of advice was our wonderful, wise pediatrician. In addition to the pointers he gave us in person, his office had a helpful service where you could call in between seven thirty and eight in the morning to ask any question without a charge. For new parents, it was a godsend. When I was pregnant with our second child, Dr. Baker shared these gems around having two or more small children at a time:

Zones of Action

First, he talked about zones of action. He said: When your first child is a toddler, all the action in the house happens between the floor and the two-foot mark. Anything interesting to them is there—toys, movement, and their parents' attention. When you have a baby, all the action moves between four and six feet above the floor because the baby is held. For a toddler who has a baby sibling, this is a big and difficult change. He suggested doing everything possible with the baby—changing diapers, feeding, and reading—while sitting on the floor. This brings the baby and the action down into the toddler's space.

Two Crying Children

Our pediatrician also gave us surprising advice on what to do when both the baby and the toddler were crying. He told us that unless the baby's head is wedged in the crib rails, always go to the toddler. The toddler will remember being ignored and make your life miserable. The baby will be fine—maybe a little mad, but that passes. I recall thinking that this advice was so counterintuitive, but it worked.

Three or More Children

One of the hardest transitions is going from two to three children. Dr. Baker didn't have suggestions for this change, so we found our own solutions. Although we were becoming efficient at taking care of little people, I underestimated the impact of switching from man-to-man, like in a basketball defense where each parent had one child to carry or soothe, to a zone defense, where one parent got two happy kids and the other parent got the unhappy one. Little things, like crossing the parking lot when you're the only parent on the errand, get harder. (I would have two hold my hands and the third hold the belt loop on the back of my jeans.) When one was sick, we had the other parent deal with the other two—but when all three were sick, we lost track of who needed a diaper, bath, or snack.

I had a tough time going to the grocery. When there were two, I would put one in the seat and one in the holding area of the cart with the groceries. Then with three, I either had a cart full of children and had to carry the groceries, or I had a cart full of groceries and three on-the-move children.

When we were in a crowded space with all five of us, Jim and I would tell everyone to be like a train. One parent was the engine, the kids were the cars, and the other parent was the caboose. Our single-file group had a parent at both ends so that we wouldn't lose track of a lagging child.

One time, I was trying to fit in a quick errand on my own with the three girls, who were all tired. We were in the back of Target, far from the front doors, and things got bad very quickly. The oldest (four) refused to sit in the cart, the second (three) was trying to run away, and the third (eighteen months) was in tears. It was getting worse by the minute.

The book we had been reading, *Make Way for Ducklings* by Robert McCloskey, popped into my mind. I said, "Let's be like ducks and go to our pond." I folded my arms like wings and started quacking as I took a few steps forward. They stopped crying and stared at me with their mouths open, stunned. Their faces were streaked with tears and snot. I was walking down the Target aisle making very real duck sounds (or so I thought). They started laughing and fell in behind me. We waddled and quacked our way out of the store.

In the months and years that followed, one would notice a sibling losing their patience, and would shout, "Go like ducks, Mom," and we would quack our way to where we needed to be. I am deeply grateful that no one had cameras on phones then, or I would have been an Internet sensation.

If there is a way to summarize the advice for the transition from one to two to three children, it is that you likely can't run errands with just one parent and the kids, and there isn't much of a break. But we adjusted. Our kids became more dependent on each other and less on us. We all survived and thrived. Advice from wise people and a sense of humor helps smooth the transition to having multiple kids.

The Kitchen as an Activity Hub

It can be a challenge to make sure homework gets done and dinner is ready in those few hours right after school. One perfect partnership for us was cooking dinner and homework. The kitchen seems to be made for both.

When I was growing up, we were expected to do homework in our bedrooms, and it was hard to find a pen or pencil if you lost yours. It was a lonely, unproductive place for me. As parents, we made the transition to a communal homework experience in the kitchen. We kept supplies— paper, crayons, pens—in a cabinet and the pencil sharpener close by. When we came in from school, I would slice apples, vegetables, and cheese to put on the kitchen table. The kids would unpack their homework, spread it out on the table, and start snacking as we chatted about our days.

I could stand at the counter, chopping vegetables to

cook or washing dishes, and the kids would be just a few feet away. They could call me over to look at something they didn't understand; make an observation like, "This dingo has crazy fur"; or tell us all something about their day, like what funny thing happened at lunch or what they sang in music class.

Cooking and spelling words are a perfect match. Whoever was practicing their words would sit on a stool by the stove, and Jim or I would read off the word and have them spell it back to us while we prepared dinner. It was a beneficial way to do two things at once, and we were present without being in the way.

As they got older and homework was less interactive, there were days when I would get my laptop out of my bag and sit at the table with them, finishing work that I had started earlier. Same result—I was present but not hovering, and we made the best of our time together.

As they went into high school, each child found different places to study. We have a tree in our yard with a perfect branch that you can sit on, and that was a favorite spot. On the floor with our dog, Fergus, was another popular place.

Even when they attended college and moved into professional work, each found ways to be productive in spaces and company that worked best for them.

Skip Fancy and Matching, Choose Soft and Warm

If you have ever tried to wake a small child on a Chicago winter morning and talk them into taking off their warm pajamas to put on school clothes, you know what a challenge it can be.

Here's a secret: the best kids' clothes, along with the best pajamas, are colorful, soft, and comfortable. When our kids were little, we diligently bought pajamas for sleeping at night and interchangeable pants and shirts for the day. We didn't buy a lot of outfits where the top had to match the bottom and instead tried to find colorful solid pieces that could easily be mixed and matched.

One night, tired of the morning battles, I put the kids to bed in fresh clothes—warm turtlenecks and soft pants. In the morning, all I had to do was tuck shoes on their feet. It saved so much time; we avoided unhappiness with being cold as they changed and arguments about what to wear. There were even a few times that the kids insisted on wearing the top or bottom of their pajamas to school instead of clothes, and no one seemed to notice.

Passing Clothes Down and Clothing Freedom

Another place we found efficiency was in buying solid-color, gender-neutral clothes. This made it easier to share between children, and if one outgrew a size that another couldn't wear yet, we would just set them aside in a box with the size written on it until we were ready to use them again. We also bought socks in bulk in the same colors, so a lost sock wasn't an emergency. (We kept the socks loose in a clear bin, and the kids had the option to choose two socks of the same color or two different ones. They still fondly remember "the sock box.")

When they were little and quickly outgrew cleats and snow boots without wearing them out, we kept boxes of footwear and would check the boxes before we went to buy new ones.

Lastly, we kept their clothes in plastic bins on bookshelves that they could reach easily. (Dressers were too hard for them to open on their own when they were small.) Since they could see their clothes and get them on their own, they could make their own choices.

When the choices are simple, it is easy to turn over decision-making to the kids. Barring shorts in winter, we generally let them decide. This saved time for all of us. Although Bea was still easily distracted—we would find her dancing in her underwear or sitting on the steps with one sock on and the other nowhere to be seen—one distraction was better than four.

BATH-TIME HACKS

Baths can be a black hole for time. My parents advocated for a single bath for each child and felt that showers were for teenagers. That takes a lot of time. Here are things that we did that would have horrified my parents but were time-savers for us.

Showers and babies. We figured out that the fastest way to get a baby clean was for a showering parent to carry the baby in and then pass the baby out to the other parent waiting with a towel.

Group baths. For toddlers, all at once was our

solution. We'd put two or three at a time in the tub, and they would play while we took turns washing hair and bodies.

Swimming, sprinklers, rain. There were some days in the summer when they would go swimming or play in the sprinkler or the rain until they were soaked. It wasn't exactly a bath, but it got most of the day's dirt off.

Communal showers. Between the ages of two and six, showers are fun—like standing in the rain. We would put our kids in the shower and let them play. It wasn't exactly a bath, but it was fun and got them fairly clean.

BASKETS, LAUNDRY, AND ORGANIZATION HACKS

Growing up, my siblings and I were expected to keep our shoes in our bedrooms and put our laundry in one big hamper. That meant a trip to a bedroom to get shoes, and also that whoever folded the laundry would need to sort stacks by person. Jim and I started that way, but the inefficiency was striking. At first we spent a lot of time trying to find matches for socks or remember who was the owner of a specific shirt. These are the adjustments we made:

Shoe baskets by all doors. When we moved to Chicago, many of our neighbors took their shoes off at the door, and it made so much sense—less dirt tracked through the house. We bought big wicker baskets and put them by each door. When the kids came in, we'd have them toss their shoes in the basket. It looked a little tidier than a pile of shoes, and it reduced wasted trips to other rooms. It also made them easier to find when we were trying to get shoes on four pairs of little feet.

Laundry baskets in bedrooms, by name. My mother-in-law taught her three boys how to do their own laundry when they were about ten years old and playing sports (with a lot of dirty practice clothes). We borrowed her idea, giving each child a laundry basket with their name on it. Even though the loads were smaller, each child could start their own laundry in the washing machine. They left their basket with their name in front of the machine. If someone else heard the indicator that the load was done, they would move the laundry into the dryer, and move the basket over. That way the clothes, once clean, went right back into the basket with the correct owner's name. Granted, that meant everything was washed in warm water, but we didn't have expensive fabrics that required careful laundering. Jim and I also had to check new clothes to make sure they were prewashed so that their colors didn't ruin other clothes. These small steps enabled us to keep laundry going smoothly without a lot of parental overhead.

Laundry snowball fights. When the kids were

little, we would have them help organize clean laundry. When we were all done and socks had been paired up together in balls, we would have a sock snowball fight. They were soft, so no one got hurt. It was boisterous and fun, and it was a reward after getting the laundry ready to put away.

Other stuff by the front door. We kept school backpacks, hockey sticks, and cleats by the front door. It made it less likely that someone would forget something and easier for Jim and me to check for folders that teachers sent home with class information.

REFRIGERATOR CALENDAR

As our kids grew up, their schedules started to be full of Battle of the Books, sports practice, play practice, zero-hour classes, and other extra- and cocurricular activities. We bought an office calendar that you would normally put on a desk and put it on our refrigerator door. We would put the activity with the child's first initial on the calendar. As they got older, we would have them put their work schedules, field trips, and other activities on the calendar. Nowadays, with the options for shared calendars, we might have done something electronic instead, though the visual reminder every day was helpful.

DISCIPLINE

Discipline for parents is a key efficiency strategy. It doesn't save you time in the moment, but it saves you countless hours in the future when challenges arise. These are our favorite strategies across age groups.

Younger Children: Time-Outs

Thomas W. Phelan spoke at our kids' Montessori school when they were five, three, and two. His book is called *1-2-3 Magic*, and he taught us about time-outs. I will do his talk injustice, but a key concept I remember was that an ineffective way parents usually give children time-outs often sounds like this: "One. You know I don't want to do this, but you know you aren't supposed to hurt your brother. Two. Come on, do you really want to sit for five minutes? You are better than this. I saw you hit your brother not two minutes after you did it the first time and I said no . . ."

He taught a different method. He said that once you start, there is no going back. You say, "One," and then count five seconds to yourself. If the behavior is persisting, say, "Two," while counting another five seconds. If they haven't stopped, you say, "Three," and then make the child sit in silence someplace in the house where you can watch them. They sit for a minute for every year of their age. You don't put children in their room (which can be fun), and you don't talk to them. (You don't owe them an explanation, and sometimes the things an angry person says do more harm than good.)

All the parents listened that night, and one timidly raised her hand and asked, "But what if they are just whining?" Dr. Phelan replied, "How is whining any different from any other bad behavior?" I sat stunned. I'd never thought of it that way. The thing that exhausted me the most was when my kids were whining or complaining. Brilliant.

Someone else, emboldened by the first brave parent, asked, "But what if you are in the grocery?" He replied, "Why is the grocery any different from your yard or your kitchen? The stakes might be even higher than if they were in the house." Sounds easy.

It's totally not.

We went home and explained to the kids what we were going to do. The first few times, it was easy. I counted one, two, three, then placed the offender on the steps and set the timer on the oven to make a sound when the minutes were over. It was working!

Then, Bea figured out that she could easily just get up in the middle of the time-out if she didn't want to sit. So we had to put another piece of his advice into play: a parent should sit behind the offender on the steps with their hands gently but firmly on her shoulders to keep her in place. That was hard, but it worked.

Then one day, Bea decided to beat me at this game. She was three and wouldn't sit still. Every time she got up, she would immediately run, pick up a block, throw it at a sibling, then stare me down. We counted thirty-four time-outs that day. If you do the math, you'll see I had to sit behind a three-year-old holding her shoulders for 102 minutes that day, with a few minutes' break in between each time-out. I didn't say a word, and in the silence, I found resolve. I was not going to let her make me give up. Finally, tearfully, she stopped raising hell.

Aside from that day, the time-outs worked. Mostly, they worked because they were consistent. I just adapted them a little: I added the child's name, so they knew who was getting counted, and sometimes I added the infraction just in case someone was confused. ("Kate, one, for bad attitude.")

This leads me to my favorite part of time-outs. I used the category "bad attitude" for anything that bugged me that I couldn't explain but didn't want happening.

I gave time-outs everywhere. In the grocery, I would make them sit on the floor, and I would stand next to them with the cart, just staring at a shelf until the time-out was over. I figured I had a less than 10 percent chance of seeing neighbors, and my two options were to be embarrassed by having an unruly child or to have a well-behaved kid. I noticed the kids started acting up in the car, as though I was hostage to my seatbelt, so I would stop the car and make them sit on the sidewalk in the neighborhood. "Hi Christine, everything all right?" neighbors would ask as they drove by. "Fine, just fine, Bob," I would say, waving in return and standing next to my troublemaker sitting on the ground.

It paid off. If we were in a park with all the neighbors at a block party and I could see one of the kids acting up way across the field, I would call their name, they would look up, and I would put a finger up the air to count. I would do it when they acted up on the soccer field or in practice while I was there. Usually, the behavior stopped immediately.

The oldest kid we ever timed was fourteen. They had friends over and were being disrespectful. They sat quietly, and I explained to the visitors they would be free to join back in in fourteen minutes.

It works. You just have to commit to following through.

Teenagers: Options That Work

As they outgrew time-outs, we first tried grounding our kids (cutting off their privileges to go out and do social things). They didn't seem that remorseful, and they made our lives miserable by complaining while they were stuck at home with us. One day, one of the kids created a mess and frustrated me so much. At first I said, "You are grounded for three weeks." Then I had a burst of genius. I wrote a long list of chores, including a bunch of things I had been meaning to do but hadn't had time: wash the mud out of the garage, collect all the trash from the house, clean the windows on the first floor, weed the backyard, pick up dog poop, etc. I handed over the list and said, "Come see me when you are done."

What we found was that much misbehavior is fueled by anger, and nothing burns off anger like physical activity. So, as the child worked down the list, their anger dissipated and the house got cleaned. It was a win all the way around. We called this punishment "hard labor," and the rule of thumb was that you worked until Jim and I thought you were properly apologetic for your behavior. It was wonderful for us.

We also confiscated things that were important to the child, including family car keys and personal electronic devices, and we curtailed social outings—no matter how significant—if there was an infraction big enough to warrant it.

Jim and I talked to each other after particularly bad situations where one of us was on our own. The one who had been at work listened and either affirmed that the child's behavior was terrible or identified that the parent at home seemed to have an overly strong reaction. We even shared this with our kids by saying something like, "I need to talk about this with your dad, and then we will figure out what the punishment will be." There were times that we stated a punishment in anger ("You are grounded for life!") and then had to walk back from it. If we overreacted, we apologized. When we gave punishment, we explained why.

There were some times when I stole my dad's line and said, "This is one of those times when the only right answer is yes, ma'am." We didn't owe them an explanation for everything, and it was okay if the answer was just "I'm your dad, and no."

How to Tag Team as Parents

When it comes to discipline, kids are exceptionally smart. They figure out quickly which parent will let them get away with things that the other won't. When we saw increased bad behavior from one of our kids, Jim and I would strategize together: Had we stopped giving time-outs, and did we need to restart? Did one of our kids need more monitoring during a particular activity or time of day? Was there something we needed to toughen up on?

When we talked together, it helped us both adjust in parallel with each other. It was hard for our kids to put something past us with our parenting partnership.

At times, one of us would lose patience. During these moments, the frustrated parent would call out to the other to ask them to take over the situation, or the parent who was not involved would say, "Hey, I can take this," and intervene. When I was the angry parent, there were times I got mad that Jim was intervening (and I am sure he felt the same way when I did it to him). In hindsight, we always recognized that we were both lucky to have someone with fresh energy and outlook come into the situation and settle things down.

HACK RECAP: EFFICIENCY AT HOME

The heart of a "hack" is creativity, and many of these tips are nontraditional or even silly, but they worked for us.

– Consider free-range feeding for kids: let them choose the food they want when they want it

– Use zones of action to spend time with children of differing ages

– In most cases, pick up a crying toddler before the baby

– Get creative about moving around—imagine the family is a train or a family of ducks

– Use the kitchen as a hub for food preparation and homework

– Consider school clothes for sleeping to make mornings easier

– Let children choose their own clothes, and pass things down

– For bath time, consider showers for babies and group baths for toddlers, and take advantage of the rain, swimming pools, sprinklers, or group showers

– For organization, try shoe baskets by doors, laundry baskets with names, keeping other things by the door, and maintaining a visible shared calendar so everyone is clear about scheduling

– Be consistent about discipline—time-outs with little folks, chores (hard labor) for older ones—and back each other up as parents

Chapter 5

PEOPLE, YOU
NEED PEOPLE

No matter how competent and efficient you are, you will only thrive when you can summon help from the circles of people around you. Whether it's drop-offs, pickups, unexpected illness, late meetings, or unexpectedly complex work, at some point you will battle weariness and burnout. You need people to help you make a much-needed date night or late evening at the office happen.

BUILD CONNECTIONS
BEFORE YOU NEED THEM

When I was growing up, we moved. A lot. My dad started in the army and then went to grad school. Each new job brought us to a new city. My favorite part of moving was when the neighbors showed up with brownies or cookies to welcome us.

When Jim and I moved into our first house, I waited for our new neighbors to drop off brownies. And waited. And waited. About nine months after we moved in, Jim was traveling and the girls were three, almost two, and six months old. It was around ten at night, one had a fever, and I was out of medicine. I looked out the windows into the dark Chicago winter night and realized I had no plan B.

The neighbor's light was on. He was a bachelor who came home at night and parked in the garage. I would wave every now and then, but we had never exchanged names. I threw on a jacket and knocked on his door.

His name was John, and he was so gracious. He came over, sat on the couch, and watched a late show while I ran to the drugstore. We still exchange cards with him and his family—and he taught me a critical life lesson: make your own brownies. In other words, don't wait for others to reach out and extend friendship or bring baked goods. Make the brownies yourself, and go build your connections.

When we moved to the next neighborhood, we put invitations to a housewarming party in everyone's mailbox the second week we were there. We had brownies, snacks, and beer. As everyone came over, we said hello and jotted down names, partners, addresses, and phone numbers. Over the course of the last twenty years, my neighbors have checked to make sure my teapot was off, my garage door was closed, and my sprinkler was off on days when my brain was full and I forgot. They have walked my dog when we were delayed in getting home. And once, my neighbor took care of three of my kids while I was in the ambulance with the fourth, who got a concussion while racing around the neighborhood. My neighbor fed them, helped them with their homework, and tucked them into bed before I got home. Granted, I have walked plenty of dogs, kept an eye out for unsanctioned parties, and made meals for sick friends. As the saying goes, goodwill comes around.

This strategy of introducing yourself before you have

an emergency helps working parents not only at home but also in the office. I learned from one of my best bosses (Ed Dzadovsky, who I worked for in McDonald's IT) that the investment in relationships with others in times of peace was profoundly valuable later in times of need. When I started on his team, he gave me a list of people to meet. I wanted to be exceptional, so I pulled out a notepad and said, "Do I ask about their strategies? Their budget? Their projects? Their goals?"

He laughed and told me to find out where they went to school, what they loved, where they had worked, what made them laugh, and what they liked to drink. He still remembers something insightful about every person he has met, and it has helped him build the friendships in the workplace that have helped him successfully lead large complex initiatives.

YOUR WORK PEERS ARE YOUR BEST OFFENSIVE LINE

Ed taught me one of the most important lessons of my career: that my peers mattered most to my outcomes, progress, and impact as my responsibilities grew.

I had come from organizations that measured my success on my or my team's output. For the first time, I was faced with a technology ecosystem that was distributed across many teams and that measured progress by the division as a whole. It was humbling, and I made mistakes.

I had charted my team's results and success but, in doing so, had missed that ultimately none of it mattered if larger division goals involving all teams (like application deployment into production use and innovation to drive growth) slowed.

With his coaching, I began to heavily invest my time and attention in my peers. Our mutual respect grew, our business results were significantly better in my second year than in my first, and I spent a lot of time collaborating with others. I used three collaboration methods during this time, which I continue to use in my work now:

One-on-one peer meetings. I held these each week for thirty minutes. I let my peers know early if something was developing that could impact their team, and they returned the favor. This helped us identify challenges early, before they reached crisis points, and helped give us time each week to work together. We laughed a lot, and we keep in touch years later.

Business partner meetings. Either weekly or monthly, I met with folks on the non-tech side of the organization who could give me insight into what problems their teams were having so that I could realign our tech strategy to prioritize helping on the biggest-impact business goals. These meetings helped me make sure that I had a full understanding of the company's challenges beyond my own team's perspective.

Women directors group. I reached out to women who were at the director level, and we met monthly for a glass of wine to share what we heard about strategy, challenges we had, and how we could help each other. Only a few of us could do traditional networking with male colleagues— golfing, playing poker, or staying out late entertaining—so this became our way to share insight and offer support. With the support of our bosses, we met at three thirty in the afternoon and wrapped up around five.

These people all formed my offensive line. As I look back on what I accomplished, many of them were leading blockers getting barriers out of my way, and I was theirs in turn.

CHOOSING MENTORS AND COACHES

I have a love-hate relationship with the concept of "influence." For me, the word sometimes seems manipulative, and I feel the same about "networking." Yet, the truth is that how you influence others to get work done is a key part of high-achieving business organizations. The best teams get the best results because of the web of interaction they have with each other.

One challenge of working remotely (whether part-time or full-time) is that people can't always observe your work firsthand. If you lead a busy team that doesn't interact with many others, the same challenge exists. For working parents, I believe this is elevated further; it is harder to socialize after work hours with others.

One way I build my "interaction web" is by reaching out to senior people on other teams and asking for coaching. I bring them things that I think are solid, show me off well, and they have a personal, vested interest in.

For example, I reached out to business leaders in my new firm and asked them to check my content and approach for a class in which we help technologists in IT understand how our business partners drive profit for the company. (The logic of the class is that when you understand what business actions, no matter how small, contribute to the bottom line, you can better prioritize the applications or technology that supports those business actions.) The leaders were willing to give me their time because there was something in it for them; the more people understood their function and contribution, the better prepared they were to help. I got insightful editing suggestions and could make connections that otherwise were hard to make casually. It was also a chance for me to widen the audience of my work and build advocates for critical roundtables in the future where promotions and bonuses would be decided.

Another time, I reached out to our CEO's chief of staff, who I heard speak at an event. I asked him if we could have coffee and followed up on my questions from the event, and I ended up being invited to see early versions of a redesigned work-prioritization system. I shared some of our best practices with him and engaged with a part of company strategy I normally wouldn't have had a chance to be a part of.

If you don't ask, you don't get invited. If you invest in knowing about the person, their work, and their interests, you can be part of a mutually interactive and supportive web.

I once heard a wonderful saying: "No one bores a hole

in a boat they are sitting in." I believe it. Many times, I have asked someone for time to discuss my possible approach on a project, escalation resolution, or team design. It shows them how I am thinking and also earns me a supporter at the table when I bring the idea forward and can reference having shared a draft early on. It gives them a seat in my boat, and they help me keep it afloat.

After-Work Socializing

Another way I build my interaction web is to pay attention to social interactions outside of the workday. If my team does a happy hour on Thursdays each week, I let them know that I am going to try to join once a month, and then I adjust my schedule to get there.

I used to be worried about missing events because of my other responsibilities. A boss I had once said, "When you share your concerns and how you are mitigating those concerns, people become more patient with you." He was right. When I told my team that it was tough to get my sitter to stay after hours with my kids and that I would try once every month or so to be at happy hour, they were grateful for the times I could come. It became something of a special occasion; folks would joke, "Oh, this is a Christine happy hour, I can't miss this one."

Lunch Hours

While I recognized that happy hours were times to build relationships, I didn't realize at first that lunch presented the same opportunity. When I first started working flextime, I worked in solitude at my desk through lunch to get as much done as I could in the office. I didn't realize it, but I was losing an opportunity to be face-to-face with others.

Now, I spend almost every lunch hour with other people. I eat lunch alone only about once every few months. In a recent week, I had lunch with a new woman from our data analytics team, and we talked about what she hopes to do in her first year. I gave her suggestions of folks to connect with who can help her. Another day, I asked the leader from HR who runs our employee networks to meet with two other folks who have an interest in the evolution of our high-potential program. At the end of the week, I had an informal lunch with a young man who might fit into my team. The fit wasn't perfect, but he was a strong candidate and made me consider redefining the position. Each lunch had a different subject and a different opportunity.

In his book *Never Eat Alone*, Keith Ferrazzi has terrific advice about building relationships and being generous with others. I took Ferrazzi's guidance to make these hours productive and focused on people. He believes the generosity you share with others is reciprocated; I agree, and it strengthens the fabric of those who support you. Thoughtful use of your time to build relationships is as critical to your results as your deliverable work is.

THE QUESTION THAT BUILDS RELATIONSHIPS

You build relationships with others through meetings, socializing, and lunches. There is one simple question to ask at the end of a meeting with leaders or people on your team that can help those relationships develop and become stronger: "Is there anything I can do for you?"

When I ask this at the end of one-on-one meetings, it helps ground me in serving the person I just met with. Sometimes they reply that it would help if I tried to get an answer to a lingering question, reviewed a plan that was lost in email, or connected them with someone who could solve a problem. Sometimes they ask for cookies. (I am known for bringing food to tough meetings.)

When I ask, "Is there anything I can do for you?" as my meetings wrap with my boss or with leaders in our business, sometimes the result is that I am asked to drop off notes on someone's desk on my way to the next meeting. Other times, I get opportunities to work on things that are normally not my responsibility but that widen my understanding of our business and deepen my knowledge. I may be asked to proof something that is going to the board to explain a shift in strategy. I might be asked if I have any ideas about how to resolve a problem. I always follow through.

Try this question when you meet with others. It's like a gift box. You never know what the answer will be or what lies within. I have had many positive experiences from asking this question.

Hack Recap: Building Community

While work and parenting can both feel like personal endeavors, both benefit from strong communities. Your mental health is strongest when you have a supportive community around you.

Ways to build community discussed in this chapter include the following:

– Build connections before you need them

– Develop strong relationships with peers at work

– Add mentors and coaches to your web of interaction

– Socialize well, when you are able

– Use lunch hours to connect with people over work

– To strengthen relationships, ask, "Is there anything I can do for you?"

Chapter 6

SPLIT THE LOAD WITH AN ALL-IN PARTNER

The previous chapter focused on building relationships in both your work and community. This chapter focuses on partnership as a tool to make work and home life easier all around. My partner (my husband, who also works) is a central part of my reality with splitting family responsibilities. However, I have friends who have succeeded as single parents with unique support systems, as divorced parents, and in partnerships where a spouse travels constantly. I have deep respect and awe for the tenacity and ingenuity of my friends who raise happy and healthy families with partners who aren't a biological parent or spouse. Partnerships take on many forms. Through the years, I have seen parents perform better at work, with less stress, when they have a parenting partner, romantic or otherwise.

CHOOSING YOUR PARTNER

As I talked with friends about our parenting experiences and this book, one encouraged me to talk about what happens before—the part of your life when you choose a partner. I am not a counselor, and I only have anecdotal experience, but here is what I can share from my observations.

Look for signs that your partner will seek collaborative solutions early on. When you live together, do you pool funds and chores? Do you both look at a child climbing a tree in the park and think the same thing? (Some people think, How fun! I want my kids to do that, and others might think the child is poorly behaved. It doesn't matter what you think; it matters that you see the same things.)

My partner and I are different and have different tastes in a lot of things, but we line up well on how we feel about education, humor, commitment, books, social expectations, and how to have fun.

Three days after meeting Jim, I could see us at ninety, sitting on a porch and playing cards. He'd be cheating and I'd be laughing. Before we got married, we went through a program for engaged couples, and while some of it was silly, it forced us to talk about the things we realized we hadn't covered yet, especially in regards to having children. Below are just a few of the questions we had to ask each other and discuss:

– Will we have separate accounts or one?

– Will one person contribute more to finances, and why?

– If funds are split, how will we handle serious illness, job loss, or family leave?

– What is our debt situation, and what is our joint plan to address our debt?

– What kind of house do we want to live in, where, and why?

– Where will we spend holidays?

– When we have children, how do we expect to cover
  their care? With family help? With day care? With
  in-home help? With a parent at home? Will we change
  work patterns?

– What do we see as a good parenting partnership?

– How many kids do we want? By when?

– Do we want to raise our children in a faith?

– What do we think about their education and costs?

These conversations are illuminating and help identify where you match and where there might be challenges
ahead.

Most people who have been married a long time will
tell you that it is very hard. Every married couple we know
can point to a time in their life when they wanted to give
up, yet they stuck with it and chose to change and adapt.

For me, one of the biggest challenges to staying sane
was dealing with financial setbacks and pressures—unexpected big costs like furnace replacements, medical bills,
auto repairs, or economic downturns that impacted our income. Once, money was tight and I had been setting aside
funds for an oil change for my Honda. The maintenance
service was significantly overdue, and I knew I couldn't let
it go too long without doing damage to the car. I loaded the
girls into the car and went to the oil change place. I didn't
realize how stressed out I was about money until the fellow
working there told me something else had been discovered

that needed to be fixed. I burst into tears in front of a group of mechanics and told them it would need to wait until next time.

Another time we had surprise out-of-town guests come in a few days before we were due to be paid, and I took my last twenty-dollar bill to buy bagels. When I got to the bagel store, I realized I had lost the bill on the way. I sat in the parking lot and sobbed. (I did find it on the sidewalk and could bring home breakfast after all, but the difference that one simple dropped bill made was stark to me.)

While we avoided debt as much as we could and didn't pull out credit cards for things like bagels, Kate's medical issues created debt we couldn't avoid. It took us years to pay off our part of those costs.

We knew we were lucky. We had each other, everyone was healthy, and we found joy in simple things. But the truth is that financial pressures and the pressures of having children—paired with lack of sleep and having little humans dependent on you for their survival, joy, and development—create tension and stress.

The best solutions are to talk early and often to your partner, make adjustments together, and use the models in the goal-planning section. Those models can help you forecast when you expect to recover from financial challenges, including when college payments end and when medical debts will be paid off. When you can see the timing of when your financial issues will be resolved, it reduces worry and gives you a day to look forward to when things won't be so challenging.

CIVILITY AND KINDNESS

There was a study I read years ago by Dr. John Gottman—
it was discussed in the book *Blink* by Malcolm Gladwell—
about a team of psychologists who could interview couples
and within a few minutes determine with a high degree of
accuracy whether their marriage would end in a divorce or
a lasting partnership. They counted the number of times
a couple was civil to each other. That's all. Did they apologize if they interrupted? Did they support the other person's statements? Did they disagree in a respectful manner?
And so on. I was struck by the simplicity of that study.

I heard Jim Sorensen speak on the concept of conversation in relationships. His theory is that every thank
you, good morning, excuse me, I'm sorry, how was your
day, and so on is like a thread. Each time we do something
small, it adds a thread to the fabric of our relationships.
The more threads, the stronger the fabric. The stronger
the fabric, the easier it is to have what he calls "fierce conversations" about tough things like managing a financial
crisis or challenges in relationships.

On my list of goals, I try to include some goals for myself
around Jim, and many times they are the threads Sorensen
speaks of and the civilities of the Gottman study. They have
included hugging more often, doing something thoughtful
(filling his car with gas before a trip, starting his coffee before
I catch my train), leaving him a note or letter telling him how
I feel about something he did, planning a date or an evening around things he likes or people he enjoys, and reading
something he loves so we can talk about it.

I wish I could say that for me relationships just happen

easily, but they take as much attention as my work does. Setting goals helps. My friend Cara leaned on her mom for support after losing her husband. She takes flowers home to her mom, and at times she will leave work early to surprise her mom and make dinner. Cara has other family members help when her mother has an opportunity to be with her circle of friends. They are a tight and effective partnership.

Splitting Parenting Duties Each Week

Another aspect of partnering that works better with planning is splitting parenting duties.

When we first had children, Jim consistently traveled a few days a week. When he traveled, I covered everything, and when he was home, we split things evenly. It took me a while to realize that, overall, I was carrying more of the load. If I had to work short days in the office when he was gone and we split short days when he returned, I ended up with more short days (and more late nights to make up the difference). His travel also created an imbalance because his job naturally became a priority for our scheduling. My job had to adjust for it. At the time, we were making the same income.

Honestly, talking about this with him was stressful. He felt bad about being gone, and I felt like I was being a jerk to someone who clearly was a good partner when he was home. We would argue, and I would end up in tears.

Finally, we came up with the following table. It identified which one of us dropped the kids off at school, what other key things were going on that day (school pictures, a book report due, a doctor's appointment, sports practice, etc.), which parent picked the kids up and made dinner and, at the bottom, Where are Mom and Dad? As our kids got older, we would stick a copy in their backpacks so that they had it for reference.

Each of us would try to give a few weeks' notice to the other for bigger events—those critical things we needed to be present for, like trips. On Sundays, we would sit down, he would confirm his travel, and I'd confirm my big meetings. We would fill in the non-negotiable spots.

Then we would do a quick count. If I was covering seven of the fifteen spots due to his travel, it was clear he would need to cover the rest, and vice versa. It became an objective and simple solution to something that caused a lot of stress before.

	Mon	Tues	Wed	Thurs	Fri
School drop-off					
Things to remember for the day					
School pickup/ making dinner					
Practice pickup					
Where is Mom					
Where is Dad					

SICK DAYS AND SCHOOL DAYS OFF

Another aspect of coordination for working partners is managing children's sick days and school days off. When we first had kids, I stayed home with the kids when they were sick more often than Jim did. Without thinking about it, I settled into a pattern of being the one to rearrange my schedule to stay home with them. After a few times of missing two or three days in a row, it was clear that the cost of unplanned days out of the office was high to me and my work team. Project work was being delayed, and schedules were put at risk. It became clear that I needed to better partner with Jim on this.

The solution we came up with was to alternate days out of office and to plan around commitments on calendars. If I had a critical meeting on day one, Jim would cover the first day, I would take the second, and so on.

As our kids entered school, vacation days became a challenge too. As soon as the school calendar was available, we'd sit at the kitchen table and go through the year. First, we'd check our corporate calendars: did one of us already have that holiday off to cover the kids? Second, did we need to call in reinforcements and see if our parents were willing to travel in for part of a holiday period to help? Lastly, for the longer breaks, how would we share them (alternating days or clusters of days)? We blocked our work calendars for the year ahead so that we were well prepared to cover those days.

When our kids were younger, we had a full-time childcare person come to our house. When the kids were all in school, summers would require too much time off to cover with our vacation days, so we found college students who had access to transportation and hired them for childcare during those months. Supplemental part-time assistance helped make up for school breaks so we could meet our work commitments. Other friends have been able to leverage family or do childcare pools to accomplish the same thing.

One of my brothers times his vacation to be opposite of when my artist sister comes to visit his family. She helps with their kids, and he and his wife keep their work schedule. This minimizes the days they take off for their kids' summer breaks.

A friend who is a teacher covers all home responsibilities in the summer, and her wife covers most of them during the school year, so the teacher misses minimal work days.

Another friend had her parents come live with her. They shopped for homes together and found one that gives them all privacy. When her work puts her unexpectedly on a trip, she knows her son is in safe hands.

Ultimately, planning conversations reinforce the fabric of your partnership. Even if your partner is your ex-spouse, your sibling, parent, or a friend who helps care for your kids, early discussions always help.

Specialize

A key part of partnering with another person is understanding what each of you does best and how you fit together.

I had my wedding dress made by one of my mother-in-law's friends—a sweet older lady who sewed from her home. Because she was going to be away around our wedding, she made it four months in advance. Meanwhile, Jim and I decided to run a race together. My running regimen significantly increased, and I lost inches around my waist. The change in my body was such that when I put on my dress two weeks before the ceremony, I could shrug my shoulders and the whole front fell forward.

At that time, we were required to meet with a couple at church to do a couples counseling process, and I needed to get the dress rebuilt by someone else with very short notice. My stress levels were high. We were the first to get married in both of our families, so they were anxious too.

When Jim and I met with the couple from church, we took a compatibility test and returned a few days later to get the results. When we came in, they took my arm and seated me on a chair and Jim on a couch across the room. (Odd, I thought.)

With very serious expressions, they explained they had concerns about our test results, particularly one question. You see, each person filling out the survey answered the statements with answers of never, almost never, sometimes, almost always, or always. Apparently, Jim had responded to the statement "The behavior of my spouse sometimes frightens me" with "always." When they read the question and answer to us, all the stress I had been feeling came out in laughter I couldn't stop.

The pastor later told us that they recommended we not be married because we were too immature. But he thought it was funny too, so he married us and told us to be careful of how our humor comes across to others. Another bride in that moment might not have found Jim's joke funny. I saw it differently. Jim knew I desperately needed to laugh, saw an opportunity, and took it.

The lesson for me: best-fit partners know what you need. On tough days and in stressful moments, a simple gesture to illustrate that you're in this together can make all the difference.

Jim's humor, his ability to release tension with laughter, and his joy in life made him the "fun" parent. He was the one rolling on the floor saying, "Steamroller! Steamroller!" as the kids tried to jump over him. He was the one wearing a beret, explaining what he was cooking in a horrible French accent as the kids lined up on kitchen stools shouting, "Chef Pierre! Chef Pierre!" I did not roll on the floor; I cut out shapes for making crowns and helped make Harry Potter robes and wands. I was somewhat boring by comparison.

Maybe as importantly, we each took over areas of responsibility fully so that only one of us had to master them. I covered all health insurance. Jim covered all school registration and school physicals. He covered sports sign-ups. I covered clothing. He covered all shots (I am afraid of needles), but we went together to any sick visits that had us worried. We both went to all parent-teacher conferences together. We both cooked, and we both shopped for groceries. We did our own laundry and took turns doing the kids' laundry until they did their own.

It was just like in my work; there was no reason for a database expert to fully understand user design or vice versa. There is no ROI for two people both mastering everything. Even wearing a beret and cooking like Chef Pierre.

INTERVIEW: KARI VANDERVEEN, Global
CIO Hewlett Packard Ent. Financial Services

If you ask Kari about the secret of her success, she always smiles and says, "Marry well."

Kari and Scott have a mantra they have repeated over the years: "Are we doing what is best for our family at this point in time?"

When they had their first daughter, they decided that while both would work, one of them needed to have a flexible situation. At first it was Kari; she was consulting in project management, and Scott owned his own business. When she was offered a role at VW Credit/Audi Financial (which ultimately led to her role as CIO), they traded positions. Scott became the "primary person" for their daughters after selling his business and starting work as a consultant in his field. He was the first to take the calls from school if someone was sick and the first to cover school drop-offs.

She says the decisions about their roles and the adjustments they needed to make were made after much consideration based on circumstances at the time and were revisited along the way as jobs changed and kids got older. The focus was always on what was best for their family at that time.

She notes that her parents modeled something similar when her mom left her job as an elementary school librarian (with hours similar to school schedules) to go back to college to finish her degree. Kari was in middle school at the time, and she remembers her dad fully supporting her mom by taking on more responsibility at home (on top of his full-time job as a university professor) and her two brothers stepping up by doing chores like laundry and making dinner. She thinks she and Scott took a similar approach in sharing responsibilities and teaching their kids to take on age-appropriate responsibilities while working together as a family. She thrived, rising through roles at VW/Audi and moving to Hewlett Packard Enterprise Financial Services as Global CIO.

Here are three practical strategies she shared:

Kari would charge her cell phone in her home office, away from where they had dinner. (Their ban on phones at dinner lasted until both girls went off to college. She and Scott had started to relax that rule, and recently, one of her daughters home for a visit said, "Hey! No phones at the table!")

They also had a Google calendar for each person and a shared one for the family (color-coded for each person). Everyone had access to all; this helped a lot when planning and coordinating who needed to be where and when. When the kids were old enough, they could add their events to the calendar, knowing "if it's not on the calendar, it doesn't exist."

Another practical strategy they had was to have set guidelines for traveling. Over the last twenty years, travel was the challenge most likely to make tensions rise. Kari traveled extensively during the week, and Scott traveled on weekends related to his consulting business. At one point, Kari's job required her to travel over weekends to global locations and, for the first time, her situation was negatively impacting Scott's ability to do his job. Later, when they were empty-nesters, the issue arose again; they were trying to travel during the same times so they could see each other, and instead had conflicts. They talked and agreed something had to change because their mantra wasn't being met. Kari ended up transitioning to a new role.

Kari observes that there weren't many role models for what she did, and she and Scott "muddled through it." (Although she perceives herself as muddling, when I worked with her she was always unflappable and composed.)

Kari talks about letting go when they decided that Scott was the children's "primary person." He was more lenient ("yet both kids are still alive," she laughs). She recalls having a small twinge of guilt when she was home late one morning having breakfast with Scott and one of the girls came to him with a hairband and said, "Daddy, will you do my pony?" and he fixed her hair.

The toughest days, Kari says, were Mother's Day and Father's Day, when they attended their church, and sermons focused on the traditional roles of both. Yet even on those days, they would go home and ask each other, "Are we doing what is best for our family at this time?" The answer was always yes.

HACK RECAP: PARTNER HACKS

Much as Kari and Scott found the roles that were right for their family, each family finds their own way. Strategies include:

– Choosing well at the outset, and talking early about practical matters and expectations

– Treating each other with civility and kindness

– Splitting duties weekly

– Alternately covering sick and non-school days

– Specializing in certain areas so each partner doesn't have to do everything

– Nurturing relationships with other supportive folks in your life who can help you

Chapter 7

KNOW YOUR BARRIERS AND ADJUST

You are an excellent (and early) contributor. People rely on you. You have a network. You have a wonderful partner. But there are still barriers to having a family and an accomplished career, and there isn't enough open conversation about these barriers.

These are things people don't talk about—the tough truths of being an involved parent and working. The goal of this chapter is to help you go in with your eyes wide open and armed with some strategies to adjust to these barriers.

LEAVE AND ITS IMPACT

If you have led or worked on a project that was critical to your organization, you know the negative impact of losing a key player, especially if the loss was unexpected. The truth is that if you are amazing in your work, your project and your work will be negatively impacted without you.

One positive aspect of pregnancy is that it takes a long time. You have time to prepare and think things through. When I was managing projects and became pregnant, I would think about the work ahead and what I could do to mitigate risk. These are things I considered:

– Could I invest in and train junior people on the team to stand in for me in the months before my leave so that, when I left, they could cover my work (which would be a big opportunity for them)? Then when I returned, they would be ready for promotion. A win for me, a win for the project, and a win for the company as I developed talent to move into bigger roles.

– Could I set a standard for team meetings and hold tight to that standard so the team could continue without me? If everyone was very accustomed to the patterns of our work—designing, developing, testing, and doing reviews in cycles—they could continue to follow the course I set for the group.

– Could I schedule important foundational work earlier in the project than normal so I could oversee some of the riskier work, leaving the less risky work for when I was out?

These questions helped me prepare to minimize the impact on my work team. Two friends also had effective leaves with minimal impact. The first friend was in sales, and she built her team with a very strong internal sales staff to support her. Her staff was so strong that when she went on leave, she kept her "book of business" (her clients, contracts, and commission) because her support team could keep things going.

Another friend knew she wanted to transfer to a global role, so she started to collaborate with one of her sponsors before announcing she was pregnant. As she gained her sponsor's advocacy, she was able to leave her US role and, when she returned months later, start a new global role.

When you approach these leaves with care and give yourself time to prepare thoughtfully, you can reduce the impact of being out and increase the organization's willingness to bring you back in.

To Share (or Not) Your Family Plan

Sofia attended a workshop on career development and asked me, "When in the interview process do I tell the company that I am considering having a second child so I can be transparent about my availability?"

"Never," I replied.

The challenge is that it could take Sofia two years to get pregnant, and if they hire her but put her on low-risk projects because they think she could be out for an extended duration, she has lost two years of potential career growth. Or, she could be interviewed by a person who has a subconscious bias that parents of young children aren't as committed or productive as people without children or with older kids. Most importantly, have you ever known a guy to mention in an interview, "I might be out for ACL surgery in the next year or two"? The recovery time is just as long; the timing is also unknown. It's not relevant information to share in an interview, and the likelihood that anything positive comes from sharing it is very slim.

The key is for us to see the barriers like Sofia did and plan proactively for them, in private with our partner.

CHILDCARE COSTS

I was working as a technical architect when I had my first child. When Jim and I did budget planning, we figured out that the in-home caregiver would cost as much as my net take-home pay. In essence, we would make nothing when I went back to work after our first child.

During the first week of my maternity leave, a new server design was introduced that changed how we designed redundant servers on networks. I realized that if I left tech for years, I would lose the currency of my knowledge. Ultimately, that would impact my ability to manage teams, get jobs, and be compensated well. When Jim and I talked about it, we realized that though we made no money by having me stay in the workforce, we gained three things: protection of my long-term earning power, my sanity (I love my work and how it stretches me intellectually), and an example for our children of two parents who loved their work. In time, my raises and promotions changed our income-to-childcare ratio from a net neutral budget to a positive.

In addition to considering the impact on work, we thought about the timing of having our kids. By having our children close together, we minimized the impact and optimized the costs. In-home care was one and a half times the cost of day care when we just had one child. When we had two children, then three, in-home care stayed around the same cost, but day care for all the kids would have been three times as expensive. The other savings for us was that, if one of our children was sick, they could stay home with the caregiver instead of there being an incremental cost for sick childcare or us needing to take vacation time to care for them.

These were our decisions, our variables. We sat down, talked about both jobs—their potential for growth, their potential for flexibility—and made decisions about timing and childcare that fit our plan.

Realities about Jobs that Fit Flexible Schedules

I wish someone had told me that after having children, schedules never work the same again. In fact, after the challenges of leave and dealing with high childcare costs, adjusting to the limitations of a new schedule might become one of your biggest barriers at work.

The tough truth is that some professional roles fit more naturally with parenting schedules. Positions that require heavy travel or long face-to-face hours in the office are ultimately not a good fit for involved parenting. These are key aspects of prospective roles that better suit the busy years of parenting:

Travel can be scheduled well in advance and with flexibility. Jim traveled a good deal, but he would use red-eye flights to come home before the kids woke or short trips to cover key meetings so he'd be gone for as short a time as possible.

An ability to plan work and meeting schedules. Control over the calendar makes almost anything possible. This is one reason why project management worked well for me: I controlled the meeting cadences and schedules and was invested in the team being early or on time.

Individual work, like analysis or design. These tasks have high reward, and in many cases are done in solitude, meaning that teams aren't dependent on your presence.

Work you are an expert in. When you take on work that is completely unfamiliar to you, it is hard to estimate the length of tasks; you can be surprised by failure and need to have unplanned work to recover. When you are an expert, it is much easier to control the results.

Leadership when you have a strong team. See the interview with Deb Hall Lefevre in chapter 8. I agree with her conclusion that when your team is strong, they can get work done independently, and you can rely on them.

When I was at a midpoint in my career, I met a co-worker who was one of the smartest financial minds I had come across. He was working as a staff accountant. I found out that he had been a controller for another one of our divisions, and I asked why he was doing this much simpler job. In a peaceful tone, he said that his mother was ailing, and this job allowed him to take long lunches to see her in the middle of the day. He never traveled. He was always done with work early, and his boss was so grateful for the excellent work that the boss didn't mind when the accountant arrived or departed. It was the right fit.

For several years after our fourth was born, I chose to remain an individual contributor—a project manager leading teams but not managing staff directly. I had realized that this company's expectation of team managers was that they be in the office every day for nine or ten hours, and I wanted to have flexibility instead. I leaned in to my family, and I continued to be a key resource for my bosses. At a later point, when I took a role that required long hours, Jim took a simpler role in his organization to be home every afternoon to make dinner and help with homework.

When you make these choices with a full understanding of what you are gaining and why you want what you are achieving, it's a pretty powerful feeling—even if it does slow down your trajectory in work for a while. For us, the trajectory of our family was a different achievement.

PERFORMANCE REVIEWS

Communicating your achievement at work is very important. Another hard truth is that people who work remotely or work flextime can be vulnerable to the review process; they are seen less and subconscious biases about how "hard" they work or how much they work can affect reviewers. Here are some simple ways to end up with strong progress and a positive review despite being part-time, remotely based, or working flextime.

Track Your Time

One challenge remote or flextime workers can have is tracking work hours. While contribution is most important, hours worked is another key data point for organizations.

When I started flexing my calendar (working varying schedules that didn't conform to nine-to-five hours five days a week), I tracked my hours. Working on Sunday nights counted, for example. To be honest, there were times when I felt so tired and overworked but, when I looked back at my calendar midweek, I'd realize I had worked just twenty-four hours so far and my sense that I had worked a lot of overtime was incorrect.

There were other weeks that I worked forty hours by Wednesday afternoon, and because of my agreement with my boss, I could work less or not at all on Thursday and Friday. This is an extreme form of flexing, and it worked for me and my leadership.

In general, tracking your hours helps you keep an overall sense of how you are investing your time and helps rule out subjective assessments (either positive or negative). I recommend you track your time; the data is valuable for your planning and potentially valuable to your organization as well. (A simple tip for tracking is to use email or messaging time stamps and your calendar to reconstruct your day.) You can also work with your manager to see if she would like you to share the results with her on a consistent basis.

Quarterly Objectives

Hours worked is a small data point about work. A more important data point is what progress is made and what work is completed. Quarterly objectives are an effective way to set and measure goals. Every three months, I set objectives based on the calendar year goals for our team and myself. Quarterly objectives are smaller, SMART (specific, measurable, actionable, realistic, and time-bound) efforts that can be started and completed in ninety days. For example, if my annual goal is to improve project on-time results, I could make the quarterly objectives look like this:

Q1: By February 15, write a draft, and by March 15, write a final summary of schedule results for projects from the previous year. By March 30, share with boss, identifying the new target for this year.

Q2: Attend project management training in April and send follow-up to boss by May 1 identifying two concepts I will apply from the class that I believe will improve schedule control. By June 15, send observations to boss about whether applying those two concepts worked.

Q3: Using concept from class of writing change requests when business increases scope, and create template for change request approval by July 15. Be able to show written change requests in next two months to leadership by September 30.

Q4: Gather list of change requests this year, amounts, and business partners in draft review by October 20. Set meeting with leadership and business partners in November. Have a written summary of impact of the new change request process, and a recommendation for next year by December 15.

Now, at the end of the year, I have the following accomplishments to list:

– Analyzed last year's results

– Set targets for this year

– Created a template for managing scope changes

– Applied the new process and measured impact

– Shared the results with business and leadership

– Recommended approach for next year

– Resulting improvements: XX%

As you write quarterly objectives, you are checking with your manager to see if you are on track, and you are collecting detailed notes about progress every ninety days. By the time you get to the end of the year and are asked to write your self-evaluation, you have notes from every quarter prior.

Even if you get busy later in the year, it can be hard to remember what you did months before. These notes remind you of the specific progress you have made. Your year-end recap has a richness of detail and a clear explanation of your contributions.

Compliments Folder

In my email inbox, I keep a folder that I call "Atta Girl." In this folder, I save emails or notes about positive things people have said throughout the year. On tough days, sometimes I open the emails and read reminders of the progress I am making. At the end of the year, I go through these and add notes to my self-evaluation in the words of others.

Goal Progress

Every few months, I look at my annual goals from my boss. If any of the goals are no longer relevant because of a change in our business or a change in strategy, I bring it up and we talk about replacing it with something more relevant. (This keeps me from reaching the end of the year with an unmet goal that is outside of my control.)

When I write my self-evaluation at the end of the year, I follow her list in order as I note completions and impact. This makes it easy for her to see exactly what I have done, in a structure that is familiar. For example, I might write:

Goal: Agile transformation. Completed, teams effectively running process, and our last 45 projects were delivered via Agile.

Goal: Rerun maturity evaluation. Deferred per meeting in July and our work with the Integration project. Replaced with culture survey, completed in November.

The more effectively you prepare for reviews, the easier you make it for your managers to give you more responsibility, compensation, and opportunity.

Following Terrific Bosses

A final strategy for career growth and getting around barriers is to follow a terrific boss. If you have done the work in this chapter and are doing well in your role, especially if you have proven yourself and have been given flexible working arrangements, consider following your boss when they are promoted or move to a new firm. They may not always have a role for you, but if they do, it is an efficient way to continue to build on a well-oiled reporting relationship.

Not only paying attention to barriers in your career but also adjusting to take advantage of situations with fewer barriers can help you succeed both at work and home.

Interview: Kate Vein,
ClearEdge Marketing

Kate is the VP of Operations at ClearEdge Marketing. She and her husband, Mike, have two small boys. After commuting into Chicago for eighteen years, Kate led operations for a company with workers in multiple states, all collaborating remotely. ClearEdge's workforce is almost completely virtually based; 90 percent of the company's staff are parents who work remotely. She calls ClearEdge a "shining example of remote staff getting it done." Kate shares that, at first, she was concerned both about isolation and about distractions.

> **Isolation.** Kate became effective in her career through relationships and face-to-face interaction. One tactic she uses now is to set cadences for

connecting with people she works with. She finds that when dealing with insecurities or challenge areas, nothing replaces the effectiveness of face-to-face meetings, so she stacks up those meetings when she is in an area where staff is located or when staff is brought in to Chicago to meet.

Distractions. Kate believes remote work isn't for everyone. One staff person at ClearEdge—who was single, with no kids—requested a full-time office spot because she found her home environment distracting.

Manager skills. Kate says working remotely presses managers to step up their game. No longer can you measure a person's commitment or contribution by the fact that they arrive early and appear to be working hard. Kate talks about "guideposts" that she establishes with staff—the what, when, and how of their work. She plans check-ins so staff can share work in progress via video calls and conversations.

Space and childcare. To make things even more interesting, Mike also works remotely, and his company operates in a different time zone. To accommodate both of their schedules, she works on the second floor of their house and he works out of an office in the basement. She smiles and notes that sometimes they text each other during the day. Both have doors on their spaces so they can have uninterrupted calls, and they have childcare out-side the home during business hours.

Efficiency impact. Kate says the best impact has been the recovery of her commute time to spend on work or her family. The toughest impact has been the reduction of face-to-face time that she feels is critical to successful collaboration. She treats those times like a precious resource and makes the most of them.

Joy and being present. After we spoke, Kate continued with her routine, then reached out to me to follow up. She noted that since we talked, she paid more attention to her routine and said, "Not only is my commute time significantly reduced, but I'm mentally present, which is making a big im-pact on us. Often I'd commute home, rush around, make dinner, do the bath and bedtime routine, and then I'd think, 'Was I even present for my family in the last two hours?' I'd either be consumed with the rushed routine or still mentally at work or in my commute. The joys of not bringing that home mentally are significantly freeing."

Hack Recap: Tough Truths about Work-Life Balance

Much like Kate discovered isolation in working remotely, there are some realities of work-life balance that you need to work around.

– Proactively plan to minimize the impact of being out for parental leave

– Run the numbers for your childcare options, understanding the projected costs based on number of children and the value of both parents working

– Deliberately choose roles that lend themselves to the flexibility you need, and avoid those that don't fit

– Understand and track your work hours—for your own use, to see patterns in work, and to share data with your manager

– Performance reviews are essential to maintaining progress, especially for those working remotely or flextime, so keep quarterly objectives, track time worked, track compliments, and meet frequently with your boss to keep things on track

Chapter 8

ELEVATE YOUR LEADERSHIP

Having a family while working comes with barriers, and the best way to be successful in both is to focus intently on skills you can build that will enable you to lead teams and larger bodies of work. There are core management and leadership skills that you will need to succeed: building teams, helping them function at a high level by understanding their strengths and their gaps, advocating for them, delegating, developing, and coaching.

People don't talk about how hard it is to go from being the star player to the coach. It takes work, but if you are honest with your team about how it is hard for you to let go and share how you are trying, success will follow.

I was the best project manager at my company. I started out on small projects, then graduated to bigger, then extremely large projects. Teams asked to borrow me to rescue other project managers' projects that were in distress. I started sharing ways that I kept track of work and the technical standard my teams used. I became our expert, and my company asked me to manage a team of project managers.

I was a terrible people manager (at first). I assumed that since my projects were so successful, my way of doing things could bring success for other project managers. One of the first things I did was require that all project managers have status meetings in the model of mine—an hour on Tuesday mornings, with an agenda so that people knew what to expect.

My new team pushed back on these patterns. At first I was frustrated, then I swallowed my pride and just watched how they ran their projects. One of the project managers got her team together every morning for a fifteen-minute meeting to start the day, and the team quickly discussed what they were doing. She called this a "huddle." Her approach and this meeting were far ahead of their time. Now Agile scrum teams follow best practices and have meetings like this every day.

Another project manager wandered around with his coffee every morning. When I followed him, I noticed that he would drop by people's desks and chat. "Hey Bob, how was the softball game last night? Haha, that sounds funny. Gosh, any luck getting that integration finished yesterday?" and so on. He basically had his status meeting by wandering around (a management concept pioneered by the founders of Hewlett Packard years ago).

Each of them got their projects done on time and in their own style. I learned to give room to my teams for their own approach (and the joy it brought them in their work).

I was able to share new skills with them, like running escalations where problems could be triaged and fixed more quickly and presenting to business teams when we had design decisions that we needed support for. I respected their approaches that worked well and helped them get stronger in areas where they were less experienced.

Even though other people may not adopt your exact

practices, the truth is that if you can shift into a role teaching others how to do what you do, you become exponentially valuable. That is, even if I am a star player worth twice as much as an average team member, I am worth ten times an average team member if I manage a team of ten and raise their performance to my level. It's a game changer, and it's worth learning.

This chapter includes some of my favorite ways to build leadership skills and your career.

Align Team to Strengths

Extensive research has been done on the profitability of organizations when companies align employees and their unique strengths with their work. Gallup has found that these employees are more engaged, and profit of those organizations is 22 percent higher than companies with an average level of engagement.

When I first started in my career, I was on a sales team and I was unhappy. I could do all the work—cold calling, building quotes, managing orders—but it wasn't fun. My favorite days were those when we sold something technically complicated and I had to prepare a write-up of the technical architecture and the approach to implementing it. Those days when I was working on the technical approach plans, I felt like I should pay my bosses, because it was just fun to do my job.

I took a chance years ago and pitched my bosses on letting me see if I could turn that role into a full-time position in the company. They agreed to a six-month experiment, and thirty years later, both my former company and I are still doing that work. Researchers call this feeling of fun in your work "flow"—meaning when a person is in a unique situation that strongly matches their talents, interests, and experience. Everything feels easier, and results are usually very positive.

When managing teams, that perspective is critical to keep in mind. Years ago, I took over a struggling program-management team. The manager before me gave each project manager a big project and then smaller projects to fill up their days. Everyone did financial evaluations of their assignments. As I got to know my team and what they enjoyed, I found some clear divisions:

The big projects usually lasted multiple years, and because of the duration of the project, the technology didn't change much. Neither did the customer teams who were part of the projects. The project managers who loved big projects enjoyed the relationship building and challenges of large scale.

The smaller projects were normally new technologies. These projects were six to twelve weeks long and high pressure because they often involved failure of some aspect of the new design. The project managers who loved these projects loved being on the leading edge of what we were doing as a company. Their focus was the rapidly emerging and evolving technology; they perceived technical challenges as exciting and rewarding.

Lastly, I had one project manager who loved financials. Even though he was junior on the team, his analytics for projects were always on time and always a little more sophisticated than the rest. His favorite part of the week was reporting.

I took the advice of Marcus Buckingham and Curt Coffman in their book *First, Break All the Rules* and started treating each person differently. For those who loved large projects, I gave them only the big ones. For my technical adventurers who loved rapidly changing tech, I loaded them up with the small pilot projects. For my fellow who loved numbers, I asked him to take on a role doing only financials for the team. In time, the eleven people doing what they loved outperformed the original sixteen people who were all doing the same work when I started.

I got to the point of being able to help my people specialize and perform by spending much of my time with them in one-on-one meetings each week. This investment of time paid off when their results improved substantially, moving us from the last-place team in the US to one of the top teams.

At home, Jim had cut his travel back for my first three months in the role. I worked long hours to gain an understanding of the work and to adjust to my new boss. Jim's flexibility gave me a chance to say yes to every meeting, no matter what time of day it was. I could figure out where we stood as a team and start to form an action plan. It took me eighteen months to fully turn the team around, and the investment of those first three months set the basis from which I could structure my work into a flexible schedule that met the team's needs too.

Most importantly, though, my focus was on the performance, excellence, and efficiency of my team. For me, the heart of analyzing the team was figuring out what everyone excelled in and realigning work to exploit their strengths. Once that occurred, our team efficiency and performance results rose significantly. It was worth the investment of time to figure out where people's strengths existed and match them to best-fit work.

HIRE TO GAPS

One of my clear memories from growing up is of my dad going in to the hospital he worked for. It was a Catholic hospital, and he was the first administrator that wasn't a nun. The hospital had started years before as a home for unwed mothers and had become known for its maternity care. As part of his interview, he was asked to take my mom to dinner with the hospital team. She was pregnant with their fifth child—and I think that's what got him the job. I believe that night he checked two boxes on their assessment: (1) understands maternity care, and (2) is very motivated.

The hospital finally hired someone who didn't have the title of "Sister" because it was on the brink of bankruptcy, and they were desperate. My dad, who was just a few years out of grad school and had relatively light experience, was just the right salary for the budget.

My father's first challenge was that nurses were frustrated and considering unionizing. To better understand their issues, my dad started going to all the shifts, between which he slept in a hospital bed in an empty room. I remember him packing a bag and being gone, or coming home for dinner and leaving again so he could be in the hospital during the second and third shifts.

He spent time getting to know everyone's names, something that still amazes me. His commitment to talking to people and understanding their problems and what he could do about them helped hold off unionization, which would have likely triggered the closing of the hospital. I remember so clearly how hard he worked to get to know the whole staff.

Years later, he was working long hours again, this time to finance a large-scale relocation. One night, he explained to me how they structured bonds for financing, and I asked how he ever learned about the financing strategy for the project.

He laughed and said he hired well. He figured out what he didn't know and what his team needed. He hired bright people out of competitive graduate schools who were hungry for work and who had finance-oriented MBAs. He hired for his gaps. His strengths were strategy, people, and disruptive growth. To cover for his gaps, he found medical, financial, and process experts, and he trusted them to do what they were good at.

Part of this step is understanding your team members' gaps and designing the team so that one person's strengths cover another's gaps. If one member of a team completes work quickly but is prone to error and disorganization, make sure another member of the team is a thorough, detail-oriented person. If someone is diligent and thorough, pair them with someone courageous and innovative.

I was giving a performance review one year, and I shared some concerns I had with the project manager I was reviewing. He was habitually late in the morning, and it made me crazy. When we talked, I asked about his tardiness conversationally, trying to understand what we could do differently. He admitted that he was an "afternoon person." His energy hit its peak around three or four in the afternoon, and he often stayed until seven or eight in the evening, riding the wave of productivity.

We made a deal that day. I covered the early mornings, and he covered the later afternoons. It made it easier for me to make it to school pickups on time. Once we changed his workday, I observed how much he got done. His strength covered my gaps.

Now, I am open with my team about when I am at my best. I am a Monday person. I am also a morning person. (They all tell me that makes me a crazy person.) Because my week starts strong, I can solve the hardest problems in the morning, and my energy and optimism persist into the early afternoon. The downside of this Monday/morning dynamic is that, by my own assessment, I get noticeably dumber as the week wears on, especially if the week is intense. I ask folks to reschedule key meetings for when I am at my best. I show them how I adapt by saving work for Fridays that either energizes me (like reading new research or organizing my desk or files) or needs little cognitive excellence (like status reports and clearing out my inbox). When I am transparent about optimizing my time for results, I notice they are comfortable adapting as well.

Overall, when you talk openly about strengths, gaps, and how they help the team get things done, you help establish a culture of self-evaluation and collaboration.

ADVOCATING FOR OTHERS' FAMILY TIME

Whether people are on our team or not, we as leaders can advocate for them as parents. When I was writing this book, a peer shared this tweet with me:

"'We expect women to work as if they don't have children, and raise children as if they don't work.' Shout out to all the working moms who feel like they are being measured by impossible standards. I see you. xoxo"

It rings true, and there is something you can do about it. When you advocate for others, you help set new standards.

An analyst working for me needed to make a certain train to get to day care on time. My boss would regularly ask me to book meetings at four o'clock with the three of us. Knowing that the analyst needed to be at the station at five o'clock sharp, I would book the meeting to end at twenty minutes before five. I watched the clock like a hawk. If it looked like we were going to drift past the deadline, I would suggest a follow-up meeting. Each meeting, I put the analyst's area of focus first on the agenda and encouraged him to bring his coat and backpack with him. We never told the boss about day care or the deadline; I just managed to the time that we had.

A coworker needed to care for his ailing mother and would arrive late some days. If our boss (whose days were so long that he arrived in darkness and left in darkness) asked about something the coworker was working on, I would just reply, "We talked this morning, and this is what we believe our plan is." I didn't clarify if we talked on the phone or if it was a messaging exchange.

You can subtly help your coworkers manage their family and worktime, and ultimately this helps us all.

PROTECT YOUR PEOPLE

I worked for a CIO once who was an angry shouter. (I won't be naming the company in this story.) There was an outage of a critical system, and he was furious. Once we recovered the system, I apologized for the outage and explained I would find out what happened and how to keep it from happening again.

I worked with the team to figure out the root cause. It turned out a young engineer with a newborn had forgotten to renew a certificate that allowed our systems to be accessed by users. He was terrified that he would lose his job. I asked what happened, and he explained it clearly and then told me what he had already done to prevent it from happening again. To avoid a recurrence, he staggered the expiration of the related certificates so that we would never experience a full outage again, and he had met with accounting to automatically pay the renewals.

I went back to the CIO, told him what the technical issue was, and how the team had solved it. He still shouted at me. He wanted to know the name of the person who made the mistake. I declined to share it, and said, "This ultimately is my responsibility, so if you want to penalize someone, penalize me." He paused, blustered a little more, then went back to his office.

The point is, leaders need to step up and protect their teams when there is human error. There is value in protecting competent people. Everyone makes mistakes and deserves support when they recover well.

TAKE BLAME

Years ago, I led a team to redesign a disaster-recovery solution. We ran complex financial systems, and our plan was that if a natural disaster hit our data center, we would recover the data from tapes that we had stored in a different location onto backup equipment at another site (like I said, years ago). Our CIO said he would support anything with a return on investment (ROI) of less than one year, but no more. He was a tough guy, and he wasn't always kind in how he dealt with failure.

The planning was intense and ended with us giving the CIO a presentation including the ROI he expected. He approved the project, shook hands all around, and we all went back to our desks. As I was going through notes to kick off the project, I noticed that something in my spreadsheet looked off. As I dug in, I realized I had made a calculation error and our ROI exceeded his target. It wasn't significant, but it was above the limit he set.

Normally, my boss would have me bring news to him first, then my boss would go to the CIO, but I didn't want to put my boss in a bad spot. It was my error, and only mine. I walked to the CIO's office numb and nauseous. His lunch was spread out on his desk. I explained what happened, that it was my fault, not the team's, and that I would redo the assessment. He looked over the new numbers and the mistake and approved it as it was.

I went to my boss, explained what I had done, how I had gone to the CIO and apologized and fixed the error, and how the CIO had responded. The project went well and ROI was as expected. As I look back on that time, I think the CIO was surprised to get a brief, objective explanation and an acceptance of responsibility. It reinforced for me the burden and reward of personal accountability.

Delegation and Being a First-Time Manager

Letting go of tasks was tough for me. There were things I felt like I could do exceptionally well, and at first I continued to do those things. I started running out of time to be with my team and get the work done. I started to delegate tasks, and it took me a while to get it right. This is what I learned about effectively delegating:

> **The why.** The "why" needs to be part of the delegation discussion. If a report is needed to determine which equipment to shut down, the person actually doing the report needs to know that in case the report he runs doesn't reveal that information. Then he can make adjustments on his own.

> **The when.** Tasks need a due date and time. I might say "by Monday," meaning Monday morning, and someone might hear that as Monday by five o'clock or as before work starts on Tuesday. The due date needs to be based on two things: Is the person usually on time? (If not, I'd set it artificially early so that there's time to recover.) And, Was the task clear enough that it could be completed? (If not, I would set a check-in date to see work in progress.)

The who. If there is something that the person is good at and has strengths for, I share why I was specifically asking them to do the task and why I trust them. It's also important for the manager to keep track of assigned work, just in case someone forgets. Ultimately, you are responsible if it is or isn't done on time.

The how. The method by which tasks are delivered is important. Do I need to see it before it is shared? How should it be sent, presented, or saved?

The transition from star player to coach of star players is hard work, and the payoff is significant as your career progresses.

RADICAL DELEGATION

While on a panel for technology leaders focusing on innovation, I was asked, "What is your one tip on transformational leadership?" I was caught off guard, thought for a moment, and gave an honest, instinctive answer: radical delegation.

Everyone delegates. When I am in peak periods of work, I look over my normal, steady-state workload that I can define, describe, and have someone on my team take over. This normal delegation frees me to focus on the "unsteady state" of technology and people in our daily work.

Radical delegation is different than delegation. It feels different and looks different. Delegation is defined as entrusting a task to another (usually someone less senior); I used "radical delegation" to reinforce the separation and trust needed for innovation.

When I worked at VW/Audi, my focus was on our financial IT data centers in the US; I was also part of the National Diversity Council and was exposed to VW's cultural expectations around work and decision-making. Many of these expectations had their roots in the German education and work systems.

Traditionally, VW and Audi promoted long-time engineers to top positions on teams. Because of this, designers were typically older and had worked in the company for an extensive period. In addition, designs came out of Germany, and it was rare to have Americans on design teams.

As a result, VW and Audi autos were criticized for not suiting Americans (no cup holders, for example) and for being staid and uninspiring. Two Americans (J. Mays and Freeman Thomas) out of the Simi Valley–based VW of America design center were given leeway to design a new breed of car. This was a departure from tradition—in the designers' relative youth, country of birth, and work location—but the cars they designed, the new VW Beetle and the Audi TT Coupe, went on to fuel US business growth in the late '90s.

In hindsight, I can see why those innovative cars came out of a somewhat disconnected work center without involved corporate leadership and oversight.

This was an example of radical delegation. Deliberately, fully handing off a challenge or task is an unnerving leap of faith in our teams and takes leadership courage. You must remove barriers to innovation; oversight creates caution, and review creates adjustment to meet expressed or perceived expectations. An unfettered team may be joyous or terrified, but they are going to think unlike you and what got you here. And that is exactly what innovation is.

If innovation is on your list of responsibilities, you need two things: smart people on your team, and the courage to really, radically delegate to them.

AGE-DEFYING PEOPLE DEVELOPMENT

Besides delegation and radical delegation, a key part of leadership is how you develop others. As you elevate yourself in your career, measurably elevating others becomes one of the most important yardsticks of your contribution. Strategies for helping people achieve their potential work both for people on your team as well as for your children.

When my children were young, I read a wonderful book about birth order and how trends emerged in how kids at different points in the birth order behaved. The book talked about how many oldest children were academics, likely because their parents had a lot of time to spend with them and were more interested in teaching them because it was a new experience. Second children were normally something first children weren't. They were athletes or artists. The author Kevin Leman believed this was because kids adapted to doing things that gained their parents' attention. It wasn't that the second child was less academic, or the first child was inherently less artistic, but that the families started to identify children as "the smart one" or "the athlete."

My first takeaway was that parents' assessments of kids seemed to be consistently flawed. My second takeaway was that achievement is a self-fulfilling prophecy, and people can't get to what they don't aim for. Maybe most importantly, never underestimate the power of a good message. Though we might have had private concerns about our kids' academic or athletic capabilities, we expected good results from all our kids publicly, and they all are achieving terrific things.

I assess and develop technical talent in my company, and I find myself using tactics inspired by my experience and studies like this. These tactics cross between parenthood and profession:

Praise and Feedback

Whether you're talking to an elementary school student or a thirty-year-old software developer, the worst feedback you can give is "good job" or "great work." These phrases are too vague for someone to know what behaviors to repeat or to thoughtfully consider after the fact. A better approach is to be specific and personal.

For children, thoughtful and specific feedback gives pointers on what to continue to do as they grow and learn; instead of "good job," specific feedback could be "I admire the way you solved that problem using a different calculation." For team members, specific feedback on performance and on the person's relevance and contribution to the organization provides insight on what behaviors to build on in their career. Instead of "good leadership," a good piece of praise might sound like, "I appreciate the way you kept your patience when Tom went off track and how you got the group to complete the task."

Timing is equally important. When a child gets

feedback in the moment of the behavior, they can easily recognize and repeat the behavior later. When a team member gets feedback in the moment, they aren't waiting until a performance review potentially months later to hear what is working.

Not only is specific and immediate feedback clear and actionable, it can also be joyous, a celebration of progress or results at the moment the effort has been put forth.

Detective Skills and the "Why"

As a parent, you will develop your detective skills from the start. You diagnose a cry as hunger, discomfort, or loneliness. You continue to figure out tantrums, pouting, and teenage silence over time. When you pause and consider what contributed to the moment, you discern the real reason why it is a calamity that a sock is lost (it's not the sock at all but that the child missed a nap and is tired and sad about everything) or that someone else is sitting in a particular chair (the problem is less the chair and more that the child is hungry and irritable after missing lunch).

Fully grown humans are no different. As critical as it is to give feedback about behavior, it is also important to figure out why the behavior is happening in the first place. When you sense resistance to an idea like promoting a software developer to a new team, you should pause and consider. You may discern that the developer is concerned about their role in a reorganization or that they are working long hours and are concerned about the impact additional responsibilities will have on their ability to get work done.

Detective skills about human motivation help you see

situations through others' eyes, and that helps you find solutions to what is driving human behavior. An apple can solve the issue of someone sitting in a specific chair if the person involved is a hungry child. Explaining a team change in which you address workload and hours and your plans to rebalance project assignments can solve the developer's worries about workload. Time spent understanding the underlying causes of resistance can help you reframe your approach and have a better outcome.

Autonomy

When someone brings an issue to me, whether they are five or twenty-five years old, I respond the same way: "I trust your judgment and your intellect. How do you think we should move forward?"

Granted, you can't ask a five-year-old to make a decision about whether to go to the dentist. But when they say, "This puzzle isn't any fun," or, "I don't think Dad will be able to come to my game," you can flip the conversation and ask them what they think a solution could be. You could get answers you don't expect: perhaps the puzzle is too easy, or they think there is a piece lost, or perhaps the dog could come along to the game since Dad can't make that one.

Your teams can also surprise you when you put decisions in their hands; many times, they volunteer to take on more responsibility to fix an issue or identify a solution you haven't thought of. When you turn over decision-making to your children or your teams, you subtly indicate your confidence in their ability to solve problems, provide an opening for new solutions you hadn't thought of yourself, and encourage them to take responsibility for solving problems.

Families and teams are stronger and happier when people are autonomous.

Being Heard

I am always watching out for raw talent. When I was part of McDonald's corporate technology team, we had talent roundtables. A team mentioned a bright young woman in their group and indicated she still had some development ahead of her. I hadn't met her before, so I invited her to coffee.

Her managers were correct; she was intelligent and creative. We chatted about the work she did and how she aspired to be in an architecture role (responsible for the design of complex technical systems) in the long term. I asked if there was any area of personal development she was working on. She sighed and said, "They don't listen to me. I have ideas, but they don't listen."

Although her group was one of my favorites to work with and known for getting large projects completed successfully, it was full of loud and boisterous guys. She was the only woman, and she was young and soft-spoken. I could see how she couldn't get a word in edgewise. I gave her two ideas to try that had worked for me:

Change physical position. Try leaning in toward the center of the table, pushing your chair back from the table, or just steepling your hands as you rest your elbows on the surface. Sometimes physical movement distracts the group and creates a break in the conversation for another person to speak up.

Illustrate. This is one of my favorite pieces of advice. Go to the whiteboard and draw out your idea. This combines physical movement with a new visual to draw attention. You can do it silently or say, "I have an idea," then start to draw or draft it out.

A few months later, I glanced down a long hallway and saw her at the end of the building wing. She raised her arms above her head in a victorious reach and called, "Christine, I stood up!" I had no idea what she was talking about at first, and she repeated: "I stood up, and they listened!" I grinned for the rest of the day. Soon after that, I hired her into an architecture role on my team. She continues to thrive at the table and at the whiteboard, making sure her voice is heard.

Change Your Perspective

Years ago, I helped lead a large project to install computer systems in a client's office and manufacturing facility. This was in the early days of networking technology, and if you made mistakes in how you set up the cabling, it could cause the whole office network to crash.

Our team had gone out multiple times because the client's network was going down, and people couldn't work. Finally, the client team realized that it appeared to be related to their coworker Tom's workstation because, when he was out on vacation for a week, the network was problem-free. We replaced everything—his computer, his cabling, his connections to the cabling—but still the problems persisted.

One day, the client called us and sounded odd. They said, "You aren't going to believe this, but Tom just walked into his office, didn't touch anything, and the network crashed." Now we started to wonder if Tom was one of those people with a strange magnetic force. We were running out of ideas (other than Tom's early retirement).

I had an engineer on the team who walked into Tom's office and decided he needed a different perspective. He shifted Tom's chair out of the way and sat on the floor mat. He literally wanted a different angle on the problem. As he sat there, he realized the network cable ran under the mat. When anyone stepped on the mat, the prongs in the mat that held it to the carpet penetrated the cable and caused what network engineers call "noise," which disrupted network communications. We moved the cable and the problem was solved.

I tell this story often, and I apply it to life. When I can't figure something out at my desk, I go sit on the floor of my office. When I lost patience with my kids when we were stuck inside, we would go play in the rain. Teaching others how to reset perspective, whether virtually or by using physical reorientation, is a key leadership skill.

INTERVIEW: DEB HALL LEFEVRE,
Global CIO Couche-Tard

Deb ran a successful team of five doing strategic planning for financial systems at McDonald's. She loved her work, and she recognized in herself a tendency to get consumed in her job at times. She and her husband Mike's work schedules could be coordinated so they were able to cover their nine-year-old daughter's non-school hours. Deb's dad had just died, and her mom, who lived six hours away, was struggling.

She was thinking, "Life is about more than work. I want to be a good mom and a good daughter." And then her boss asked her to take on a new team.

It wasn't just a new team: it was eight times larger, focused on a technology she wasn't familiar with (data warehousing and analytics), and the team was struggling. They seemed to have a fear of saying no and, as a result, hadn't been meeting commitments. Also, the technology they developed and supported wasn't working well. The data warehouse system would often freeze when users tried to execute reports, and frustration was high. At first she demurred, concerned that she couldn't be the present mom and daughter she wanted to be. Her boss held firm, encouraging her to build a strong team, saying they would enable her to be everywhere she needed to be.

I know how the story ends—the data warehouse and insights team she built is still the cornerstone of McDonald's analytics, and she was ultimately promoted to CIO of North America and senior vice president. The heart of Deb's ultimate success lies in what she did when she took on that new team. Deb talks about how she did something she hadn't done before: she built a high-performing team she could trust to deliver. She did this in three ways.

Leadership off-site meeting and workshops. During these meetings, they discussed what they believed high performance and collaboration looked like and built a shared understanding of what that would be before they started working toward it. They also built camaraderie.

Trust. She developed her ability to trust her team—not telling them the what and the how but instead giving them the space and support to execute and doing what she could to get obstacles out of their way. She talks about how when she "stays out of the weeds," three things happen: her team has the space they need to work, she can focus on strategy, and she has time for family. Deb noted how challenging this was and that she stumbled at first as she figured out the right amount of oversight and delegation.

. . . And verify. She honed her ability to sniff out issues in a technical space she was unfamiliar with. In her words, "You can't get just out of the what and how; you have to be super clear on your expectations."

While running this new team, Deb worked a condensed workweek. For a while, she worked four days a week, and during another period she worked remotely on Mondays and Fridays. She was still the room mother in her daughter's class and could stay involved. If you ask her her secrets to parenting, she will tell you two things: load-balancing with her husband and outside help.

Deb's husband, Mike, was a pilot with seniority. That meant he could organize his schedule to fly Fridays through Mondays or do turns (where he left in the morning and came back in the afternoon). Between the two of them, they covered nearly all their daughter's mornings and afternoons. Her "village" was made up of two neighboring families who helped too, pitching in when needed. Though all their kids are grown, the parents remain close today.

One thing I will add to these notes is that Deb was a visible female leader in technology in an organization that didn't have many women senior leaders. She was generous with her time and counsel to other women in IT and maintains a strong relationship with all her former teams. It is one thing to hear people talk about how to approach challenges; it is something more powerful when you get a front-row seat to watch them do it.

Hack Recap: Leadership

While my career started with strong personal results, I learned leadership is the way to grow and share your personal excellence. Deb's interview supports the conclusion that the better you master leading teams, the more opportunities will come to you. The benefit is that many of these hacks work on team members as well as children.

– Align your work team to their strengths

– Know your team, and hire to fill gaps

– Advocate for other parents

– Back up your team if they make a mistake

– Take blame when you make an error

– If you are a first-time manager, invest significantly in learning how to delegate effectively

– To drive innovation, radically delegate

– Develop people
  – Make feedback and praise frequent and specific
  – Understand why people react and behave as they do
  – Build autonomy in others
  – Teach them to be heard
  – Teach them ways to break through challenges and change their perspective

Chapter 9

TAKE YOUR KIDS (IN)TO YOUR WORK

There is much written about work-life balance; some even suggest that there's no such thing. My work and family both bring me joy, and I have found ways to bring them together.

When our children were young, they attended Montessori school. One of the premises of Montessori is that humans love to work. Children in a Montessori classroom are encouraged to "choose their work," which for them means activities in the classroom. As a result, you end up hearing three-year-olds say things like "I love my work" as they tell you about their day.

We paid attention and talked to our kids about what we were doing in our jobs. Jim would tell them about the applications for his equipment to abate pollution and how he was able to help companies recycle chemicals to not only reduce pollution but also save costs. I would celebrate team breakthroughs, sharing how we had figured out a way to solve a problem. I would show my kids technology systems in restaurants and car dealerships and explain how they worked and made things easier for people.

We also both shared what our challenges were. Sometimes we would have bad days, and we would share our setbacks and the mistakes we made. We shared our recovery process, too, being honest about things we did to regroup and move forward.

Jim and I believed that we needed to let our children see into our work life as often as possible so they could understand why we did what we did. While we did not take them into our offices, we amplified the concept of including children in work with these ideas.

Homework and Work-Work

As our children grew and could do their homework mostly on their own, we would open our laptops at the kitchen table and work in companionable silence. If they needed something, we were right there.

Sometimes I would ask, "What are you working on?" or "How is it going?" and they would share with me. They often asked me the same questions, and I would show them the network diagram I was evaluating for weak points, the presentation I was building and how I was trying to find good visuals to explain things to my business partners, or the spreadsheets and graphs I was looking at for data insights to help me solve problems. We both tried to show them how things they were learning (writing, mathematics, learning about ideas, critical thinking) connected with what we did in our jobs.

We wanted to give relevance from homework to work-work and help them see the crossover between the things they were solving and work that adults did.

Recovery from Missteps

Another part of bringing our kids into work was sharing how we recovered from missteps. I told my kids when I made mistakes, like how I lost my temper and wasn't patient with someone at work. I would explain how things were going badly with a team or a project. I'd also explain how I apologized and what I was trying to do about it to improve things going forward.

These conversations mirrored how we handled mistakes with the children themselves. When I lost patience with my kids and shouted or got angry, I would collect myself. I'd look them in the eye and say, "I made a mistake. I was angry and shouldn't have shouted, and I am sorry." When they observed us apologize, reset, and behave differently, they were learning not only behaviors that would help them be good parents and good spouses but also ways to be good coworkers and good bosses.

There is power in an honest apology to a family member or a coworker. A simple "I was wrong" with no defense (no "I was tired," no "Bob was late with his analysis and it frustrated me") is honest. What I did was just not good. Period. I know a lot of adults who don't apologize to their kids, but if they don't see us do it, how can we expect them to do the same? Dealing with setbacks and being responsible for your part in the setback is part of the humility advocated for in countless leadership books.

Sometimes parenting helps us be better bosses and coworkers, and vice versa. I think when parents are humble about mistakes and growth, their kids are more comfortable making mistakes and adjustments too. I know that talking about ways that I wanted to improve helped me focus better on those changes at work.

Achievement and Progress

Another key parenting moment is celebration of progress. Whether it was either of us sharing that our teams earned a new project to work on, Jim explaining a patent he owns, or us talking about how a conference paper or presentation was received, we shared our progress with our kids as well as the challenges and hard work that preceded it.

Our hope was that our celebrations (usually at the dinner table) would help them tie the hard work and the preparation to the results.

Preparation

When I was getting ready to leave one day, one of my kids said to another, "Must be a big presentation," as she nodded toward me in my favorite suit.

They had heard me do dry runs on many presentations and talks. They helped me organize materials for workshops. And they helped me choose outfits for big days. While we did this, I explained what I was doing and why. I told them that the preparation was as much a part of the work as the big day was, and I drew parallels: I packed my briefcase the night before with everything I needed, much like they packed their bags before a soccer game to make sure all their gear was clean and ready to go. Likewise, I started preparing for a big presentation a few weeks before so that I could practice and adjust even if other work got busy, just like they needed to start the research for papers well in advance in case a game bus was late getting back to school or other assignments came up in class. This also meant that my work became a parenting moment as opposed to something I was doing without them.

Interview: Kim Moore,
Former President of Coates US

Kim is passionate about women and the difference that education makes. Following are notes from our conversation on her experience.

Neither of Kim's parents had college degrees, and her childhood was filled with challenges. She followed her mother's path, getting married, having kids young, and struggling through marriage failure. Because this life—taking care of her kids and working in roles with limited income potential—was what she grew up with, she didn't see anything different than this at first. But she became interested in earning a degree when she topped out, reaching the top classification she could achieve without having a degree. Over five years, she worked full-time and went to school part-time, patching together changing work schedules, long commutes, and childcare. Her last semester, she took five classes while working a four-day, forty-hour work-week to complete her degree in time for graduation. She graduated with a nearly perfect GPA and went on to study coding languages, running large teams at McDonald's and, ultimately, the North American division of Coates.

Kim's years in school were tough. She woke at four in the morning, when she could think most clearly and her kids were still asleep, to do homework. She color-coded her notebooks and file folders to match the color of her textbooks, finding that simple things like this saved her time and reduced errors. When asked what her girls remember, she laughs and says, "They remember the 'crazy,' and doing their own laundry when they were nine." She recalls that when she finally graduated, she was so sick from being worn down that strangers were passing her cough drops during the ceremony.

During that time, Kim said she learned what to let go. Her mother-in-law would leave articles on how to keep a cleaner house on Kim's kitchen counter, and her own mother talked to her about being home with her daughters if they were sick. Kim stayed the course, left the house as it was, and finished her degree.

What is striking as you talk to Kim is how she sees her education in a wider frame. She talks about her education leading her to a professional job where, for the first time, she learned to have healthy relationships with a wide range of people who wanted her to learn, wanted to share their knowledge, and had respect for her and others. She said that experience gave her the clarity and courage to leave a bad marriage.

Kim's goal was that her two daughters would have a different life to see than she did, and they would never find themselves in the situation she found herself in. Both daughters have degrees; Kim notes, "They have a really strong work ethic, likely from watching me."

Kim remarried a number of years ago, and her husband Brian bought her pearls to celebrate both daughters graduating college.

Like Kim, when you work while raising a family, you create a unique opportunity to show children how to succeed in their work in the future. Everyone better understands concepts when they can observe the concepts play out.

Hack Recap: Taking Children (in)to Your Work

– Build and share a positive outlook on work based on how you make a difference and make progress

– Do homework and work-work together, driving parallels

– Share stories of failure and recovery

– Share stories of preparation

– Share progress and the work behind it

Chapter 10
TAKE CARE
OF YOURSELF

You are the foundation of your career and part of the foundation of your family. Ways you stay healthy and happy have an impact on those you lead—and those you love.

Humor Renews Us

We were in church one weekend with all four kids, and the youngest, who was about two, slipped and hit his head on the bench. We sat near the front so the kids could all see, so I had a wailing toddler on my hands right in front of a big church. I scooped him up quickly; he was facing out from me so people could see both of our faces as we walked down the center aisle to leave. Halfway down, he opened his eyes, realized we were leaving, and said a heartfelt, "Yesss!" The whole church laughed, and so did I. This parenting stuff is not for easily embarrassed people, and it is certainly easier when you laugh.

The same thing happens on teams and in families—when we laugh and welcome humor, it gives everyone a chance to release stress. Although this suggestion is simple, it can be hard to remember when times are tough.

Sleep Block Planning

At book club one night, a neighbor who worked in the nearby urgent care was talking about a flu outbreak. Others were talking about how contagious the strain was, yet she was chirpy and healthy. I asked her how she avoided what others were considering unavoidable, and she told me that she was relentless about getting eight or more hours of sleep every night. It made me realize that when I burned the candles at all ends—staying up late to rework project plans, getting up early to get diagrams ready for architecture review—I could feel my throat getting scratchy and a cold starting.

The cost of an illness to a working parent is high, so staying up late to finish a project plan and then getting sick is rarely worth it. Having a good project plan and getting eight hours of sleep is better than a great project plan and six hours of sleep.

It is easier to meet the goal of eight hours of sleep when your children are older. When they are small, it is far more complicated. One thing we did as a couple early on was alternate who got up with the baby and make allowances for big meeting days. For example, if I had a meeting I had to be sharp for, Jim would cover the whole night.

Those nights looked like this:

	9PM	10PM	11PM	12PM	1AM	2AM	3AM	4AM	5AM	6AM
Baby		Sleep	Sleep		Sleep	Sleep		Sleep	Sleep	
Jim		Sleep	Sleep	Feeding	Sleep	Sleep	Feeding	Sleep	Sleep	
Christine	Feeding				8 Hours of Sleep					Feeding

156

We would reverse the pattern when Jim had a key day that he needed to be sharp for. On nights when we were both headed into normal days, we alternated, and this allowed each of us to have at least five hours of uninterrupted sleep:

	9PM	10PM	11PM	12PM	1AM	2AM	3AM	4AM	5AM	6AM
Baby		Sleep	Sleep		Sleep	Sleep		Sleep	Sleep	
Jim		Sleep	Sleep	Feeding			5 Hours of Sleep			Feeding
Christine	Feeding		5 Hours of Sleep				Feeding	Sleep	Sleep	

We had a quick conversation in the evening to confirm what the plan would be for alternating our coverage of night feedings. It also helped that one of us would go to bed earlier than the other. During this time, the two of us slept on offset schedules to make the most of sleeping times. It helped us share the load of overnight parenting and do our best to stay sharp during the day at work. Sleep builds resiliency.

Sleep and Its Impact on Results

Years ago, I was working on a large team to set up a manufacturing software system for a manufacturing company. All thirty of us on the consulting team had a dedicated room (called the war room) where we kept our laptops and worked together. There were two weeks left before the planned go-live of the system, but we had three and a half weeks' worth of work to do. The new software would change how the plants and financial systems were operated, and it was set to happen over a holiday weekend when workers were out. We were all working around the clock and were starting to realize we were going to fail.

On a Thursday, the CIO came into the war room. She told us to stand up and hold our coats and our car keys. She told us to leave our laptops and other gear. She said: "You are all tired. I am sending everyone home, locking this room, and shutting down access. Go home. Hug your children, sleep, read a book, eat good food, laugh with friends. Recharge, and come back here renewed. I hired you all because you were the best and brightest. Right now you are all tired, and that makes you average. I need you to be who you were at the start of the project. See you on Monday." We were shocked. What was she thinking? How would we ever finish?

We went home, rested, and came back. And we caught up in those last two weeks. We made the go-live date, and I have never forgotten the lesson that the lack of sleep drops the quality of our work and that the addition of sleep can solve problems. When you find yourself weary and running out of time, consider doing something nonintuitive and sleep so that when you wake you can solve problems effectively.

Outsourcing Other Tasks

Money was especially tight when we had our first three children. I was working nearly every minute that I wasn't with my family and trying to stay on top of keeping the house clean. Every time that I suggested we hire a service to help us, Jim would say, "We can cover this ourselves. I will help." But, if he got busy or forgot, then it either fell on my shoulders or I ended up feeling like a nag as I reminded him. We would argue about it; I was getting worn down, and he was getting frustrated. After one particularly hard week, I made this proposal: "Let's write down what needs to be done each week, and let's put our names next to what each of us is going to do. If after four weeks the cleaning isn't done, I am going to call a service and we aren't going to talk about it again."

Four weeks later, I called a service, and we have had one ever since. I wish we could have afforded to have the house cleaned top to bottom, but since funds were tight we had a short visit to help with some cleaning that was particularly time consuming.

I have seen friends outsource all sorts of things through various services or other outside help: driving kids to practice, making dinners five nights each week, watching triplets through the night, lawn care, window washing, top-to-bottom house cleaning twice a year, clothes shopping, laundry, grocery shopping, homework help, and pet care, to name a few.

Some of these things are expensive and were beyond our reach—but the heart of the situation is that, if there are things you can afford to have someone else do and they give you time to be an involved parent and a top employee, they can be strategic decisions that help you keep your sanity. The key is asking yourself, What are my priorities? What brings me joy (and what doesn't)? What does my budget allow?

Outsourcing Chores . . . to the Kids

When the kids started to grow up, summer presented challenges. With four kids, it was a lot to ask a college-aged sitter to come up with ideas to keep everyone busy, so I came up with a solution to keep them busy and take some of the weight off my shoulders.

Most nights, I'd write a list for the kids for the next day. It often included walking to the park, reading a book, or hugging their dad. I tried to make it whimsical enough that everyone was curious to see what I put on it each day. Hidden in the whimsy was a rotating list of chores—help with cleaning the house, yardwork, and taking care of the dog. My primary goal was to give some structure to the day, but the unintended consequence was that chores that used to greet me and Jim at the end of the day were completed.

One day, I added some responsibilities for cooking, leaving a simple recipe and ingredients on the list. It was an effective adjustment. All of our kids have cooked since they were about ten years old and continue to do so now. The results weren't always good, but they turned out well enough most the time. They each developed a love for the kitchen and a confidence that comes from figuring out how to cook on their own.

Ultimately, the whimsy and variety of tasks kept my kids excited about the lists and the work, took some pressure off the babysitter to fill their time, and helped our house run smoothly.

Balancing the Load of Parental Support

A lot of research evaluates the emotional load of caring for others. When that emotional load is shared across both parents, the impact can be significant, no matter the age. When parents deliberately try to strike a balance in caring for children, it helps both share the weight of emotional support.

Little Guys

How many times have you seen a child scrape a knee and run to their primary parent? When I was growing up, it was almost expected that an injured child ran first to their mother (and then, in my family, to my dad, who would use butterfly bandages to patch us back together). When I had my own children, we'd go on long walks or outings to the park together, and when one of our kids fell or was hurt, they would look around quickly for the closest parent and go there. It created a simple and effective balance in our parenting workload. When both parents do the little things—feeding, changing diapers, baths, bedtime, home-work, school pickups, being room parent, and answering questions—it sets a lifelong pattern of the child going to whichever parent is closest or the best fit.

One challenge we had with sharing the load at this age was Jim's beard. Every winter, Jim would grow a lumber-jack-worthy beard. The growth happened over time, and the kids thought it was fun that their dad was furry like a bear. The first winter, when he shaved it off, our oldest daughters (two and one at the time) didn't recognize him.

Suddenly, the balance we had established, where they went to us evenly, had disappeared. They cried when he went to pick them up, and it took a few days for them to match his voice with his new smooth face.

The next winter, I told Jim he needed all three girls in the bathroom with him when he shaved. We have wonderful pictures of the four of them crowded into a tiny bathroom, with the girls grinning and watching their dad. This started an annual tradition of Jim shaving off his beard in outlandish ways, sometimes leaving mutton chops, sometimes a Fu Manchu mustache. We gained some laughs and kept our parenting balance.

Middle School and High School

When our kids were in middle and high school, there were times when they used one of us as their go-to. To paraphrase Mary Pipher's book *Reviving Ophelia*, young women want to set their own path as they become adults. "Own path" usually equates to a different path than the women they know—mainly, their mother. Dr. Pipher writes about how fathers are essential to their daughters' growth as their daughters form their own paths. We didn't force them to talk to both of us together when there was an issue; we gave them a choice. And they chose Jim. A lot.

To paraphrase Dan Kindlon and Michael Thompson in *Raising Cain*, many teenage boys are more comfortable talking while not making eye contact. Jim and I adjusted how we talked to our son. I talked often with him when we were driving, and I got him started on taking walks with me when he was frustrated. (He still walks now when he needs to work out ideas or problems.) Jim talked to him often while shooting baskets and other activities that had them both physically active.

Jim and I would check in with each other and share what we learned and what we were worried about so we were in sync about things to watch out for and progress that was made. We were both prepared to take a call from school if something developed or to respond in an effective way if pulled into the conversation. Jim and I shared notes and didn't force group conversations.

College Students and Adults

When our kids were in college, and in the years following, they seemed to choose one of us for our subject matter expertise. One of us is the tax guru, the other the healthcare guru. We are both experts in the foods we make; Jim gets calls about bread and salmon, while I get calls about salads and pastas. We notice they lean on us for personal guidance about their work, graduate school, and relationships and seem to have a sense of just who they need and what they hope to hear. We now share good news when either hears it, and there are some things we keep to ourselves.

HEALTH AND CARE

Taking care of your physical body is another part of caring for yourself. I am not the best example of this. In fact, it's one of my weaknesses. But I have found that, when I work out, I think more clearly, sleep better, am more patient, and can carry heavy toddlers and groceries better.

At times, I have had to scramble to find exercise options that fit. When my kids were very small, I would throw on my running shoes when Jim was home and go run for twenty minutes. I couldn't plan it because I wasn't certain of our schedules, so I just did it when I could.

When they were in elementary school, I found a gym that offered classes at five in the morning, and I would slip out while they were sleeping, work out for forty-five minutes, and come home right afterward. When they were in high school, I took classes on the weekends and during the week after dinner. Even now, when my work hours run long during the week, weekends are my heavy workout times. It's not perfect, but exercise helps keep me sane and healthy.

In addition to looking for exercise options that fit my around work and life, and I try to keep a full water bottle in my car and toss apples and oranges into my bag when I am on the move so that I have something healthy close at hand.

Our health helps our work and our families. It's not selfish to fit in exercise; it is a basic need for our performance in both settings.

Favorite Pregnancy Hacks

Pregnancy creates an even more important need for self-care and drives a need for creative solutions. These are odd things I learned by being pregnant four times. Please take this odd collection of advice with a grain of salt, as any woman who chooses to have three kids in three years is likely partly mentally unstable.

Have them close together. For us, this was part of the strategy. The cost of a nanny was per year, not per child, so we took advantage of the cost savings. Our children (at least the first three) were very close in age, so their interests and lives were similar—similar bedtimes, soccer schedules, and favorite exhibits at the zoo. We were already carrying and packing a diaper bag, so adding in a second diaper was easy. Also, we were short on sleep and used to having a limited social life, so there were a lot of efficiencies. On the subjective side, our daughters grew up almost like they were triplets, and they remain close to each other to this day, pulling their brother tightly into their circle.

Pregnancy is not an illness. Insurance and doctors want to treat it like one, with mandatory checkups and tests, but the truth is that you own the experience. I did see midwives (who delivered in hospitals, so I am only partly new-age), and they were vigilant about me staying fit and not gaining too much weight. Their counsel kept me healthy so that my deliveries went well, and my recoveries went even better. Here is a little-known fact: if you are not using pain meds and have kept yourself hydrated, you don't have to have an IV while you labor. For a woman in a hate-hate relationship with needles, that was all I needed to know.

Hair bands are awesome. As your middle swells, you can loop an elastic hairband through a buttonhole in your pants or skirt to expand your waist by an inch or so, reducing the need for early maternity clothes.

Privacy is awesome. With that hair band thing working for me, I didn't tell my coworkers about my pregnancies until fourteen weeks for my first, and twenty weeks for the ones that followed. It gave me more time in private to plan and to get my projects and work into good condition for me to be out for a while.

If you get nauseous, pay attention to triggers. I got sick when faced with grilled chicken. (Who gets sick with something so healthy? Apparently, me.) A certain fast-food restaurant's home fries, which I normally couldn't stand, settled my stomach right down. This coping mechanism helped me stay on my feet during my first trimesters, which always involved an unsteady stomach.

No one notices what you are wearing. When you are pregnant, folks think about different things than your outfit. I had limited funds, and so I had three outfits that worked for the last stages, and I just wore them in a row, over and over.

Naps. I got overwhelmingly tired in the middle of the day. I napped where I could. Sometimes that was in a parking lot in my car, and when I had the luxury of an office, I napped with my head on my desk. Those fifteen-minute catnaps were restorative.

Stay fit. When I was at my most fit, my deliveries went better. It's a pretty physical process, and strength and fitness make a difference. It helps the recovery as well.

Living within Your Means

Worrying about money caused stress for Jim and me. We learned early on that to stay happy, we needed to live within our means. If we didn't have the money to buy something, we went without. We found happiness without some trappings that were common in our generation. Here are some of the ways that we adapted.

A Practical House

Our goal was to optimize our space and have it be functional for our needs, so we used our house in some odd ways. These were spaces we either used differently than was common or adapted to be more effective for our kids.

Playroom (living room). Most houses have living rooms with nice furniture for gatherings. We couldn't afford furniture and needed a place for our kids to play. The living room was the biggest space, so we used that for toys. We kept a small table and chairs, chalkboards, toys in bins, dress-up clothes and costumes in a basket, and books and art supplies where they could easily be reached. This way, the kids were on the same level of the house as our kitchen, and

Jim and I could keep an eye on them from a distance while they played on their own.

Gathering room (living room). Later, when our kids were headed into middle and high school, we let the teenagers take over the room. We kept board games and puzzles on the shelves and put the house TV in the room. We put down hardwood flooring, replaced the toys with couches and chairs, and added glass-paneled doors to the room. The glass doors muted sound but still allowed for subtle parent oversight. Since the floor was wood, they could take food and drinks in, and it was easily cleaned.

Library (dining room). While most houses around us had dining rooms that were used for special occasions, we repurposed the space. Using inexpensive materials from a hardware store, we covered the walls in bookshelves and kept the family books there. Two big pillows went on the floor by the windows, and our kids would sprawl there and read in the sunlight. We had a table in the room that was used for art projects or as a homework space and comfortable chairs for reading. Our kids learned early on that if they were reading, we would almost never interrupt them to do chores. It was a safe zone, and so the space was used a lot. Our dog eventually took over one of the pillows by the window, and at times I would find the kids reading books to him in the fading light of the afternoon.

Open pantry. We built a simple pantry in the kitchen that was open and made sure that food was on lower shelves so they could reach. This helped the kids take care of themselves when they were hungry and gave them the option to choose for themselves from an early age.

Kids' bedrooms. All three girls shared one room for years until they started wishing for privacy. Then we had to alternate who got a turn with their own room. When they were under the age of six, they all slept better when they were close to each other. It seems counterintuitive that a baby in the same room as a toddler is a good idea, but the toddlers grew to ignore the baby when it woke, and the baby seemed to sleep longer with someone else gently snoring in the room with them.

We also put mattresses on the floor at first so it was easy to get in and out of bed and so the kids wouldn't get hurt if they fell out of bed at night.

Since we live in Chicago, where the winters are long and bleak, these beds also became indoor trampolines for jumping and dancing on days when we couldn't get outside for exercise. We took off the closet doors and added shelves with clear bins for clothes and socks so they didn't need us to get things down for them. Toys were kept in baskets—easy for them to pick up and put away.

When they were teenagers, a lot changed. Beds had frames, and they didn't jump on them anymore. We had the doors back on the closets, and our kids wanted privacy. Also, they were slobs. We implemented four rules when they were teens: no food or drinks in their rooms; they had to clean their rooms right away if they got smelly; deep cleaning would be done roughly every month; and Mom and Dad could come in at any time to check things out. Then, Jim and I would keep their doors closed.

I am sure my mother will gasp when reading this section, because she had me and my siblings make our beds daily and clean our rooms every weekend. For me and Jim, the energy we lost trying to clean up something that didn't seem to cause harm wasn't worth it. There were some gross discoveries, but nothing that couldn't be cleaned up.

Family Dinner (and Conversation)

When I was growing up, my father had to build a kitchen table because the ones in the stores weren't big enough for a family of nine. He went to a junk shop looking for materials and found an old bowling lane. He took the wood and built a table (which we immediately slid glass salt shakers down as soon as he put it in the kitchen). My parents asked us all to stay at the table until everyone was done eating, and then we would be excused. It took me a while to realize that what they wanted to do was have us spend time together. I have strong memories of talking around that table (we still do when we go back to my parents' house) and laughing until late at night some evenings. The dinner table was what helped form the bond between me and my siblings.

When Jim and I had kids, we decided that making an event of family dinners at home would be a great way to live within our means. Each night, Jim and I made dinner. Per our established free-range feeding rules, if one of the kids didn't think they would like what was for dinner, they could take a taste of what we made, and then get something they preferred. Or, if they had been eating something else just before, they didn't have to eat; they could just join us at the table. Once when our son was three, he had just finished an apple and was sitting at the table, not eating. Jim said, "You can go play if you like." Our son replied, "Thanks, Dad. I think I will just stay for the conversation." And he did.

As our kids grew up, we adapted. Technology was banned at the table (for parents too). If the week had been hectic with practices, rehearsals, or games after school, then we would start to plan and announce, "Hey everyone, we are going to have dinner together on Friday because everyone will be here." And then everyone knew to be home or delay social plans.

Another thing Jim and I did was pay attention to the books kids were reading for classes or Battle of the Books (a reading competition for middle schoolers). We would read or reread the books and bring them up at dinner. We talked about the ideas in the books, how authors approached things, what we liked about characters, and so on. We joke that it was "family book club." In fact, it was a way to bond with our kids when they were reading something they didn't enjoy and to show them that we were interested in what they were doing. If one of them discovered a book or author they liked, we would talk about it at dinner.

We talked about politics and the world too. Jim and I would start a conversation about funding for a local homeless shelter, a speech we had heard, or an issue on the ballot, knowing that they were listening. As they grew, the conversations got deeper and could go on for hours.

Conversation and etiquette are critical professionally. A key part of your professional presence is how you handle yourself at a business meal. Family meals can be effective tutorial times where you reinforce good etiquette and help your children build their capability of social conversation and discussion so they can succeed in future professional settings. Having dinner at home is a frugal practice, but one of our richest experiences.

Family Walks

Another affordable activity is walking as a family or doing simple things together. On Sundays, we would go to one of the local forest preserves or trails and walk. One of my favorite pictures shows my kids in tall grass with the dog. Jim and I had stayed up on the trail, and they were cutting through a meadow. You can just see their heads and shoulders and the tip of the dog's tail and head.

The kids would complain sometimes, but those outings were a terrific way to clear our heads and enjoy each other. We saw an owl one cold morning in winter when we were walking a loop in the woods. We saw turtles in mating migration—hundreds had come up from a marsh area to lay their eggs and were crossing the path. We found frogs and toads, and we saw foxes and coyotes on cold mornings. Some days, we saw nothing and the kids complained. Even then, at least everyone moved. To this day, when the kids come home, we all go walking around the neighborhood and paths close by.

We had other outings as well. One tradition we had when they were little was to bundle everyone in their pajamas and blankets in the car and drive around looking at Christmas lights and decorations on houses. Sometimes we would all go to the grocery together—not to shop for the week, because that would have been stressful, but to shop for dinner that night. Simple outings didn't cost us anything, and the change of pace was good for all of us.

Social Life

We were one of the first couples in our circle to get married and have kids. We quickly found out that going out was expensive. To join our single friends, we needed money not only for the dinner, concert, or game—but also for childcare. Plus, we were going to be away from our kids, losing some of the valuable time we had together.

We started inviting over neighbors who had kids the same age as ours. All the kids would play and we'd order pizza, share wine, and enjoy each other's company. Our five-year-old daughter introduced us to some of our best friends when she met their daughter in kindergarten and announced, "Our families need a play date." We did, and they have been part of our lives for twenty years. We found great ways to socialize over the years:

> **Halloween candy swap.** All the kids gather at a house and trade candy they don't like for candy they do like. Parents celebrate surviving the night together.

173

Let's put on a play. Older kids organize younger ones into practicing and performing a play. (Our youngest was an elf that looked like Elvis one year, and that is all I can remember of that play.)

Impromptu cookout. Parents pull their grills out into the street, and everyone grills whatever they have for dinner that night.

Impromptu game and pizza night. Two parents start talking on the porch about something, grab a beer, and end up calling over spouses and children. A few hours later, someone orders pizza, and then everyone is playing games and bedtime sneaks up on everyone.

Alternatives to Going Out

Dining out is expensive, so we found ourselves doing creative things as an alternative.

School pickups. On the way to school, we had to pass several restaurants, and our kids would ask about stopping, but the budget didn't support it. I started packing apple slices and playing music on the way home, and we'd munch and sing joyously. (My kids were just recalling my playlist from the drive, noting that it was the first time they heard The Doors' "Peace Frog" and Nirvana's "Smells Like Teen Spirit").

Dates. Jim and I would get beer, tuck the kids in

bed, then sit on the porch and talk or play cards. It was different enough to be on the porch that it felt like an event, but we were close enough to hear when someone awoke and needed us. Not very glamorous, but within our budget.

Volunteering. When our oldest child started high school, she volunteered at a homeless shelter with her class on Thursday mornings. She came home one day and told me there was a problem, and she solved it. She explained that school didn't go to the shelter on Thursdays between the AP tests in May and homecoming (the end of September), and the shelter was left without volunteers. "Good news," she said. "I asked if you and Dad could be certified as volunteers to oversee students, and they said yes. I told them we can be there this Saturday for training." That's how Jim and I came to chaperone a rotating group of teenagers for eleven years on Thursday mornings at five thirty. At first, we couldn't afford to bring all the donations for breakfast, so we supplied manpower and our daughter organized other students to bring supplies. Over time, as our finances improved, we could provide help and supplies. It was rewarding and grounding. When we felt like we were struggling, Thursday mornings helped us see how lucky we were.

Summer activities for the kids. Many of our friends had their kids in summer camps that were wonderful and expensive. Jim and I scoured the park district, bookstores, and library sites for free activities and were first in line on the sign-up days. We found musical performances, reading contests, authors talking about their books, line dancing, parties at the village public pool, and my kids' favorite: one-dollar old movies at the theater in our town once a week.

Birthday Parties

Our kids were invited to a lot of friends' birthday parties. In most cases, the hosting family would rent a theater or party place, and the business would prepare food and activities. We couldn't afford these types of parties, so we got creative.

We often did scavenger hunts where the kids searched as a team. We would give them one clue and let the birthday person read it. The clue might say, "Brrr. I am chilling here with the cheddar," and they would chatter together and figure out that the next clue was in the refrigerator. The next clue might say something like, "Rub-a-dub-dub, three men in a . . ." and they would race upstairs to the bathtub. Each time, they would let a new person read the clue. We set up the hunt to take them up and down the stairs in the house, outside to the mailbox, and outside again to the bird feeder. The treasure was a package of seeds.

Everyone got to paint a flowerpot—the little red clay ones from the hardware store. While the pots dried, we would have cake (a simple one we baked the day before with our kids), and then we would fill the painted pots with gardening soil and have each child plant seeds.

The planted seeds and pot were their party favor, and

the whole afternoon was within our budget. I once had a little girl (who, the month prior, had taken the group to a concert in a limousine) throw her arms around my legs, hug me, and say, "Mrs. Stone, everyone says you do the best parties." This made me smile, because our whole budget was less than one of the concert tickets.

These simple parties created a lot of upsides. We got to sit on the floor and paint pots, bake a cake together, and laugh as the kids figured out clues. It also helped our kids see two parents living within their means and to see us dealing with the social comparison with composure and self-awareness for who we are.

Kid Talk about Budgets

Birthday parties were just the start of open conversations about money with our kids. Jim and I wanted to help them understand fiscal responsibility at a young age, and we thought it was important that they see the thought behind our financial decisions. We wanted them to see how we gave up one thing so that we could enjoy another and that there were things that were important to us, but maybe not to other people, that we saved for. We were frank about budgets with them:

> **Gifts.** As our kids became old enough to under-
> stand budgets, we would tell them what we bud-
> geted to spend on their birthday or Christmas
> presents. They could decide if they wanted one
> more expensive present or multiple, less expensive
> presents. Sometimes they wanted something be-
> yond the budget, and they would pay the difference

with money they had saved on their own. These conversations were enlightening and gave them the control and understanding of the impact of choosing something expensive.

Choices like education. One day I was driving my youngest to school, and he said, "This car is a junker." He was right: it was ten years old, with a hundred and fifty thousand miles on it, and it was kind of loud. I explained how much a car cost, how much a year of high school tuition cost, and how his dad and I felt about education. And, yes, I did wish I had a quieter car, but we made the choice to save money on that to pay for school instead.

Cash versus debt. We were transparent about things that we purchased and how long it took to save. When our kids wanted something, we didn't say we would buy it and they could pay us back; instead, we helped them figure out how they could save for it and then helped them buy the item when they had the money. Our hope was to begin giving them examples of financial management when they were young.

Clothes. When they had a dance or needed shoes for a sports team, we would tell them what we could contribute. They could choose—did they want to find something more expensive and pay the difference, or did they want to buy something in the range we set? I shopped in thrift stores for myself and at secondhand clothing sales for them when they were young. We talked about looking unique and saving money by doing so.

College tuition. We didn't want our kids to graduate with debt, so we helped them find good schools and programs. We also expected them to contribute significantly to their tuition while they were in school. Each was expected to work full-time during the summers and pay us for their share, which ended up being most of what they made for the summer, before the fall semester started. Their contribution had two impacts: it lowered our costs, and it helped them feel a sense of connection and sacrifice. One daughter, after getting a low grade on a paper, said, "I am paying too much money to get a grade like this." She ended up earning an A for the semester.

It seems odd to talk about this in this book, but living within our means was essential to having kids and working. Had we pressed for a much higher standard of living, we likely would have had to sacrifice our time with them. We wanted to be with them, and we wanted the professional accomplishment of working and contributing to our companies.

One rainy day, when we were in the kitchen doing homework, one of my daughters said, "Everyone in my class has been to Disney World. A lot more than once." And one of her sisters replied, "Yes, but they don't have Fergus" (our dog).

Hack Recap: Take Care of Yourself

This chapter covered a lot of ground. Ultimately, your holistic health is the foundation of both your family and your work performance. Invest in yourself, because you are worth it.

- Use laughter to recharge, at home and at work, and take time to enjoy joy

- Get enough sleep to stay healthy and smart

- Plan "turns" waking with an infant with your partner so the person with the harder workday gets the best rest, or so you divide the load equally

- Outsource less critical tasks to others to free your time for what is most important to you

- Use kids as help, especially during the summer when they have more time and can get bored

- Plan and work with your spouse to share the emotional work of parenting

- Pregnancy hacks:
    - Consider having kids close together
    - Advocate for yourself medically
    - Use hairbands to extend the size of nonmaternity clothes
    - Delay sharing the news of your pregnancy to use the time to plan
    - Watch nausea triggers

– Nap, anywhere
– Stay fit

– Live within your means to keep stress as low as possible
   around finances:
   – Repurpose the space in your house for children—
     playroom, open pantry, etc.
   – Use family dinners as a social and learning hour
   – Go for simple outings, like walking together
   – Socialize with other families (no babysitters needed,
     and similar interests)
   – Find alternatives to spending money on entertain-
     ment—snacks in the car, dates at home, volunteer-
     ing, and free summer children's programs
   – Get creative, and stay simple with birthdays
   – Talk to your kids about money and decisions

Chapter 11

YOU'VE GOT THIS

Susan, the VP in my first story, said she never knew a successful working parent. But she does. She knows me.

What would the future have held for her if she could have understood team strengths, measured results by output instead of presence, adjusted, adapted, and appreciated hacks that her team used to find unusual and creative solutions?

It's not just that I would have found even more success with our company; she would have too. This advocacy for work-life balance is a virtuous circle. We support team members so they can be high performers, and our teams and companies are more profitable as a result. At the same time, we give team members space and energy they need to raise future generations of thinkers.

Besides understanding work and life, each of us can gain strength, composure, peace, and focus when we breathe. In those moments of silence, when you collect your composure, remember: you've got this.

You already had insight, ideas, and a great work ethic. Now you have hacks to help you fast-track your way to saving time and getting good results.

Breathe. Use hacks and best practices. Stick Post-it

notes in this book, fold the corners down, or tag sections that work for you. Try something small, then build.

Be early and be excellent. Set and measure your goals. Use every chance to be extremely efficient. Lean on your community at work and at home. Form and nurture your partnerships. Be realistic about your barriers, and knock them down or work around them. As your career progresses, be a leader and do what you can to help others and build a high-performing team. Bring your kids into your work, and please take care of yourself. You are the foundation of all of this.

Share your hacks, and share these. If you meet me and have questions, I promise to make time. If you are located close to me or I am near you, and you have a book club or group at work, I'm in.

The world is a better place with good kids and good companies.

You've got this.

BOOKS I LOVE,
AND WHY

Following is a list of books I love for business and parenting and my personal summary to give a sense of why these books work well for me, in case they might be good resources for you as well.

First, Break All the Rules. This book by Marcus Buckingham and Curt Coffman came out of their (and Gallup's) work understanding highly engaged and productive teams and their managers. The key idea is that managers who are most effective seem to consistently approach leadership differently than you might think. The book is practical and easy to read, and I apply its ideas in my own work.

The Growth Mindset. Carol Dweck out of Stanford wrote this book, which crosses the parenting and work domain. The heart of her premise is that intelligence is not fixed, and that those with a positive orientation to failure (which it is part of the process of improving) will have stronger performance and can grow their intelligence.

The Read-Aloud Handbook. Jim Trelease is a researcher who studied the positive impact of reading out loud to children. He advocates reading at a much higher reading level than the children can read themselves. His research shows that listening to complex vocabulary words and sentence structures raises children's literacy. He includes reviews and lists of books he recommends. This book was a treasure for us.

Raising Cain. Written by Dan Kindlon and Michael Thompson, this book helped me understand my son and boys in general a little better. One of my favorite stories was about a teacher who taped a four-foot square on the hallway floor. If someone was starting to misbehave in class, she said, "Take five," and they jumped rope in the hall for five minutes. It was just enough time to take the edge off, and the student was able to return to the classroom. In many cases, boys jumped more often than girls. This helped them deal with the sedentary classroom setting and avoided traditional negative reinforcement.

Reviving Ophelia by Mary Pipher. Some folks I have recommend this book to say it is sad, but I found that is has a good deal of applicable insight. Some of my favorite points are about how critical fathers are to their daughters' development, how daughters finding themselves just want to be unique (which usually means "not like her mother"), and how playing sports can have profound positive effects on a young woman's life and perception of her body.

The Birth Order Book by Kevin Leman. This book illuminated patterns that develop because of birth order. One point we took to heart was that if the first child is academically oriented, the second child in many cases will be artistic or athletic. This has a lot to do with children inherently recognizing how to gain their parents' attention from a young age. We tried to not label our kids ("the smart one" or "the soccer player") and treated them all like they were very smart (though we weren't always certain that was the truth). It helped us be better parents to four and kept us from falling into traps. It was also a great book-club book that made for terrific discussion.

"Women and the Labyrinth of Leadership." This Harvard Business Review article by Alice Eagly and Linda L. Carli summarizes practical ideas for retaining diverse members of a team. While it is focused on women, I have found its relevance to include diverse team members in general, and it gives good counsel for managers.

The Defining Decade by Dr. Meg Jay. Although written about thoughtfully planning your twenties, the book holds thought-provoking insight into the advantages and costs of decisions made early in career and family life.

Presence by Amy Cuddy. While her book and TED Talk set off a storm of academic challenge, her voice appeals to me. I have done the "power poses" she recommends, and they make me feel more settled and in control before big talks and big meetings. Perhaps experts don't understand the science—but the optimism, pragmatic insight, and potential work for me.

DISCUSSION GUIDE

I belong to multiple book clubs. My neighborhood group offers an opportunity to read things I wouldn't have normally chosen myself and socialize and laugh with women who live near me. At work, we often have book and article discussion events to share content and talk about how it can be applied to our teams or our business challenges. I even belong to two two-person book clubs. One is with a daughter who lives far away and who shares my interest in organizational design and its impact on productivity and on innovative ways technology impacts teams. We both read the same books and talk for hours about ideas. The other is with a friend who is a writer with a hectic schedule. We connect when we can and share new things we have uncovered.

GROUP QUESTIONS

My hope is to include discussion questions here that you can use with a group, whether in your work community or in your nonwork community. I hope you find hacks to share that make you all happy and more productive.

What practical advice surprised you, and are you going to try it?

What insight did you read and think "not for me," and why?

What part of work and parenting do you think people don't talk about enough?

Where have you found your best ideas or advice for your work and family dynamic?

Is there something that has been a game changer for you that the book doesn't talk about? Share it.

Is there any advice in the book that would horrify your parents like some of it horrified Christine's mom?

What do you think the generational dynamic is that drives some of the social expectations around parenting?

Do you think that gender biases around parenting roles will change in your lifetime? Why or why not?

What do you wish your boss did that could help you more?

Everyone has their own way to gather their thoughts, reset, and think about the future. If the first part of setting goals is clearing your mind and being able to think clearly, close your eyes. Where are you and what is around you that makes it possible for you to think clearly?

On Your Own

Here are questions on self-reflection, for moments of quiet and forward planning.

Where am I now with work?

Where do I want to be in five years? (Think of your potential role, compensation, work content, hours, and location.)

What small things can I do in the next year that puts me on a path toward the five-year goal?

Partner Questions

Lastly, this is a section on things to discuss with your partner. When Jim and I were young parents, he would find interesting books (usually in airport bookstores) about parenting or child development and bring them home. We'd both read them, and then talk about which theories we thought could work for our family.

Where are we now?

Where do we want to be in five years? (Think about

children, finances, work, and how you spend your time.)

Is there anything we need to change to get there?

Are we happy?

Is there anything we can do to add joy?